Therapists
Who Have
Sex
with Their
Patients

Treatment and Recovery

THERAPISTS
WHO HAVE
SEX
WITH THEIR
PATIENTS

Treatment and Recovery

Herbert S. Strean, D.S.W.

BRUNNER/MAZEL *Publishers* • New York

Library of Congress Cataloging-in-Publication Data
Strean, Herbert S.
    Therapists who have sex with their patients: Treatment and
recovery / Herbert S. Strean.
        p.   cm.
    Includes bibliographical references and index.
    ISBN 0-87630-724-1
    1. Psychotherapist and patient—Sexual behavior.
2. Psychotherapist and patient—Sexual behavior—Case studies.
3. Psychotherapists—Mental health.   4. Psychotherapists—Sexual
behavior. 5. Psychotherapists—Counseling of.   I. Title.
RC480.8.S755   1993
616.89′023—dc20
                                                                    93-17864
                                                                        CIP

Published by
BRUNNER/MAZEL, INC.
19 Union Square West
New York, New York 10003

Manufactured in the United States of America

10 9 8 7 6 5 4 3 2 1

To my sons
Richard M. Strean, Ph.D.
and
William B. Strean, Ph.D.

with love

Contents

Preface

For over 25 years, the major part of my professional life has been devoted to teaching, supervising, and treating mental health practitioners. One important dilemma of psychotherapy that virtually all of my professional colleagues continue to discuss with me is how to respond to their patients' sexual fantasies toward them and how to cope with their own sexual feelings toward their patients.

The anxieties, discomforts, and temptations that most of my students, supervisees, and patients share with me are not unique. Ever since the formal inception of psychotherapy, clinicians have had to cope with the sexual stimulation that the therapeutic situation activates in both participants. Although no two therapeutic relationships are identical, because each patient and therapist brings his or her own special dynamics, history, and adaptive mechanisms to the treatment situation, all mental health professionals are obligated to monitor their sexual desires, experience them fully without acting on them, and control them without pressuring themselves or their patients to deny, suppress, or repress sexual feelings and fantasies.

When I was a beginning therapist, I tended to inhibit, deny, and repress erotic feelings toward my patients. I find this to be true with most beginning practitioners in the 1990s. And this was also how one of the first psychotherapists in history dealt with the sexualized transference-countertransference interaction. When Freud's colleague, Dr. Joseph Breuer, noted that his patient, Anna O., lusted after him and wanted him to father her baby, he stopped her treatment and abruptly went off on a second honeymoon and had a baby with his wife.

Dr. Breuer, like many current mental health professionals, did not recognize that his patient's erotic desires were essentially displaced childish fantasies that she harbored toward her own parents. He probably did not realize either that he was turning his patient into an attractive but forbidden mother figure—his mother's first name was Bertha, as was Anna O.'s (a pseudonym for Bertha Pappenheim).

Inasmuch as we therapists are "more human than otherwise" (Sullivan, 1953), there is always the temptation to view the patient's falling in love with us as sexually titillating and narcissistically enriching. However, when, like Breuer, we do not recognize that the patient's sexual transference is a replication of his or her neurotic problems and start worrying about having an affair with the patient instead, we are distorting the patient's productions and seeing ourselves unrealistically. Worrying about acting out sexually with a patient usually disguises our wish to do so. It also reveals that we have desires to abdicate our role-set as interpreter, clarifier, and facilitator and want to become the patient's lover instead of his or her therapist.

It has been my consistent observation that when clinicians fail to help their patients talk in detail about their sexual fantasies toward them, they are usually working overtime to renounce their own wishes to have an affair with these patients. The inhibited therapist, who, in my opinion, is often excessively moralistic, is so frightened of the wish to act out sexually with the patient that he or she avers in effect, "Sex does not exist here." This practitioner fails to appreciate the infantile nature of sexuality, does not see how infantile sexuality always plays a dominant role in the individual's neurotic conflicts, and is not aware of how and why the patient and therapist are distorting each other. In effect, this therapist is like a phobic child very afraid of libidinal wishes toward parents and parental figures.

Through my intensive study of this phenomenon—the unconscious meaning of a therapist's renouncing the sexual dimension of psychotherapy—I have come to realize that this professional is really a sexually stimulated human being who is hostilely shunning the libidinal component in the therapeutic interaction. The sexual dimension of treatment is avoided by him or her because it is so tempting to act out, but it also appears very forbidden. In reality, the puritanical, moralistic therapist is actively inhibiting what the therapist who has sex with patients is acting out. The differences between the two are not so great!

Although the inhibited clinician and the one who acts out sexually with patients are both trying to cope with much anxiety, both are human beings who are suffering a great deal. We mental health professionals tend to behave much more punitively toward those colleagues who act out sexually with their patients than toward those who squelch their patients' emotional spontaneity. We tend to be much more nonjudgmental and accepting of those professionals who inhibit their patients' sexuality, who fail to fully appreciate their patients' humanness, and who retard their patients' growth than we are toward those colleagues who have affairs with their patients. Yet, neither the repressed practitioner nor the sexually acting-out practitioner is substantially helping his or her patients! In my opinion, it is an open question as to who is hurting the patient more.

We psychotherapists have a strong tendency to repeat history. Freud, who abstained from having sex with anybody for a good part of his adult life, was very critical of his colleague Carl Jung for having affairs with two of his female patients. Avowing that the psychoanalyst should behave like a surgeon who has no feelings at all toward patients, Freud came close to championing the notion that the clinician should repress sexual interest in the patient. Although he was also very critical of another colleague, Sandor Ferenczi, who hugged his patients, Freud might have been more successful in the treatment of his teenaged patient, Dora, if he had acknowledged his own wishes to hug her.

I have worked with many therapists who, like Freud, have been uncomfortable with the sexualized transference-countertransference. I have also worked with therapists, like Jung, who, although fewer in number, have acted out sexually with their patients. I have come to realize that these latter therapists need as much understanding, supervision, and treatment as their counterparts; however, they have not received it. They have been demeaned, denounced, and in many cases, destroyed, instead. Although professional clinicians tend to assert that they want to understand and empathize with their patients rather than condone or condemn them, their overt responses and underlying attitudes toward their colleagues who "exploit" and "abuse" their patients sexually have been essentially hostile, unempathetic, and punitive.

What is lacking in the mental health literature is a serious study of the dynamics and treatment of psychotherapists who have had sex with their patients. Who are these therapists? What motivates them to turn their patients into sexual partners? What about the interpersonal lives of these clinicians outside of the consultation room? What is the nature of their sexual lives outside the consultation room? Are they having satisfying marriages and enjoyable relationships with their children? What about their personal histories? How did they fare in their psychotherapeutic or psychoanalytic training? What about their relationships with their therapists or analysts? The answers to these and other questions have been essentially shrouded in secrecy but are of enormous interest to members of the helping professions and perhaps of interest to others, as well.

An axiom of psychotherapy is that the patient must be compassionately addressed and related to with empathy and understanding if she or he is to be genuinely helped. However, as I indicated, clinicians who have had or are having sex with their patients are, for the most part, demeaned, detested, and derided by colleagues. Because they have not been compassionately studied, their numbers do not decrease and the problems they pose to clientele, to professional organizations, and to themselves tend to continue.

Just as antisocial patients who hurt others and themselves need thorough understanding and skilled therapy, the recalcitrant therapist needs a similar response. Therefore, I have decided to write this book, which I believe will be the first major work to thoroughly, objectively, and compassionately study the mental health professional who has had sexual contact with his or her patients. Through intensive case studies that will describe in detail their therapeutic encounters with me, the motives, dynamics, life-styles, and psychopathology of these psychotherapists will be revealed. In addition, I will also try to demonstrate how I used myself in the therapeutic situation with these clinicians so that their psychological difficulties could be resolved and their sexual acting out with patients could be given up.

Throughout this book I take the point of view that the clinicians under examination are very conflicted human beings who need intensive understanding and treatment. In several respects they can be likened to other patients who have sexual problems, such as those individuals who have extramarital affairs, participate in sadomasochistic orgies, or engage in various forms of sexual molestation. Similar to the benign understanding and compassionate treatment that clinicians offer to patients involved in these maladaptive sexual practices, this book will present the same perspective in examining therapists who have sexual encounters with their patients. I will try to expose common themes in the internal and interpersonal lives of these *"therapist-patients"* and also try to demonstrate some of the commonalities in their treatment encounters with me. I will attempt to show that these individuals have severe problems with their own sexual identities, have to cope with a great deal of sexual anxiety and guilt, and are essentially lonely and depressed men and women. I will also endeavor to explain why these therapist-patients utilize the confidential, intimate, and trusting setting of psychotherapy to act out their sexual conflicts and by so doing are really showing their antagonism, albeit unconscious in most instances, toward the practice of psychotherapy.

In Chapter 1, "Sex in Psychotherapy," I review several dimensions of the problem before us. I discuss some of the features of the psychotherapeutic encounter and demonstrate how the interaction between therapist and patient frequently induces sexual excitement in both partners. I also consider who is psychotherapy's modal patient and who is the profession's modal therapist, so that I can show that those who participate in the treatment situation may be more prone to sexual acting out than the general public.

In Chapter 1, I also discuss why the issue of therapists having sex with patients, a subject overlooked for many decades, is now receiving attention in many places—in the theatre, in professional organizations, in magazines and newspapers, in novels, and elsewhere. I link this current concern with changes in society, particularly shifts in the role-set of women. Finally, I conclude Chapter 1 with some thoughts on the uses and abuses of sex in many relationships, implying that sex between psychotherapist and patient is not vastly different from many other maladaptive interpersonal struggles.

Chapters 2, 3, 4, and 5 contain four case studies, that is, each of these chapters will be devoted to the presentation of a psychotherapist who was in treatment with me and either was having sex with a patient or patients on entering treatment or began having sex with a patient or patients while in treatment with me. Each of these chapters describes the therapist-patient when he or she arrived for a consultation; the problems presented; crucial aspects of the therapist-patient's history, current family, and interpersonal relationships; past personal therapy and training; plus other pertinent data. As I examine the sexual activities between therapist and patient, I highlight the feelings, sexual fantasies, dreams, and transference reactions of the therapist-patient under study. As I mentioned, I also discuss my own therapeutic interventions and the patient's responses to them.

The four practitioners under study are three males and one female. This ratio parallels my own experience with sexually acting out therapists and the experience of others as well. It appears that many more male therapists are reported to engage in sex with their female patients than female therapists engage in sex with their male patients (Barnhouse, 1978; Bates and Brodsky, 1989; Gabbard, 1989). (There is very limited literature on homosexual liaisons between therapists and their patients.) To protect confidentiality, all of the identifying material on the therapists under study and their patients are disguised.

In the sixth and final chapter, I attempt to show the common dynamics in these subjects and some of their common responses to my treatment of them. After demonstrating that the therapists in this study have severe problems with their sexual identities, come from pathological family backgrounds, have dysfunctional marriages with many sexual conflicts, and experience many other unresolved problems, including a deep antipathy toward the practice of psychotherapy, I suggest how psychoanalytic training institutes and psychotherapy training programs can do more to help troubled therapists cope with their severe anxieties, pervasive conflicts, depression, and guilt instead of acting out sexually with their patients.

ACKNOWLEDGMENTS

There are many individuals who have been extremely helpful to me during the preparation and writing of this book. First, I would like to thank my wife, Marcia, for editing and typing this manuscript. In addition, she was always available to listen to my ideas and contribute many of her own. Second, my sons Dr. Richard Strean and Dr. Billy Strean, who are my favorite critics, helped me clarify many of the issues discussed in this volume.

Mark Tracten, President of Brunner/Mazel, and Natalie Gilman, Editorial Vice President, have been very encouraging and supportive throughout this project. It is a real pleasure to be associated with them.

Finally, I would like to thank the subjects of this study who enriched my understanding of human behavior, helped me become a more accepting and empathetic practitioner, and demonstrated that learning how to do effective psychotherapy is a never-ending process.

CHAPTER I

SEX IN PSYCHOTHERAPY

Ever since the formal inception of psychotherapy as a profession, psychotherapists have had major difficulties in monitoring their sexual wishes toward patients. In Freud's inner circle, Otto Rank turned his analysand, Anäis Nin, into his mistress. Ernest Jones, Freud's biographer, spent a good part of his career fending off accusations that he sexually molested young patients and had sexual intercourse with older ones. Sandor Ferenczi believed that his patients needed physical comfort; therefore, he openly fondled their breasts and hugged them frequently. Carl Jung had prolonged affairs with several of his patients, including one who became a psychoanalyst (Grosskurth, 1991).

Sexual activity with patients by the pioneers of psychotherapy has been more than replicated by their followers and con-temporaries. In the April 13, 1992 issue of *Newsweek* magazine, it was well documented that a spate of cases involving sexual liaisons between patients and therapists has come to the public's attention in the last decade (Beck, 1992). Although at least 10% to 20% of those mental health practitioners who have been queried on the subject acknowledge sexual activity with their patients, their numbers are probably higher. Many clinicians, despite being granted anonymity, are frightened to tell the truth because they fear retribution (Gabbard, 1989).

Although the percentage of psychotherapists having sex with their patients has probably not decreased since Freud's day,

1

and may have even increased, the interest and concern about the issue has intensified. There is now a rich literature on the subject clearly demonstrating the profound and deleterious effects that are inflicted on the patient who has been sexually seduced by the practitioner. Numerous articles and books in the professional and nonprofessional literature have provided indisputable evidence that the patient who has sexual relations with his or her therapist emerges full of emotional scars. Often the victim, usually a woman, appears similar to a battered child who has been emotionally abused and sexually exploited by a parental figure (Bates & Brodsky, 1989; Freeman & Roy, 1976; Leonard, 1983; Rutter, 1989).

In contrast to the laissez-faire attitude that was shown toward clinicians like Jung, Rank, Ferenczi, and Jones for their sexual improprieties, today's therapists who have sexual liaisons with their patients are subjected to law suits, loss of their licenses, disbarment from professional organizations, and other retaliatory measures. How can we account for both the strong shift in concern about therapists having sex with their patients and for the dramatic reversal in response when they are discovered?

During the past three decades numerous phenomena have coalesced to account for the dramatic modification in concern and response to clinicians having sexual liaisons with their patients. Probably one of the most influential factors is the feminist movement (Chesler, 1972). Sparked by the leadership of NOW, the National Organization for Women, and by other social activists, women have been consistently speaking out against sexual harassment and exploitation in industry and elsewhere. Recognizing that they are not compelled to submit to a subordinate, demeaned role at the work place and elsewhere has helped them to be more assertive as patients in psychotherapy and to feel freer to question "therapeutic harassment."

Concomitant with some of the successes of the feminist movement has been a reconsideration of sexual practices and sexual roles in society (Buunk & Driel, 1989; Murstein, 1978). Women are refusing to be treated as "objects," whether it be by their spouse, employer, physician, or psychotherapist. They are demanding a mutual relationship of two equals at home and work, and this mature, legitimate demand has been heard by mental health professionals.

As the revolt against sexism has become a powerful phenomenon in our society, concern has been expressed about the possibility of a latent sexism in the practice of psychotherapy (Karasu, 1980). The alleged sexism in psychotherapy may be reflected in the finding that the vast majority of practitioners who have sex with their patients are male therapists exploiting female patients (Gabbard, 1989).

As discrimination against women has been discussed in and out of psychotherapy, some basic Freudian postulates have also been reconsidered. One of the most important notions to be questioned has been Freud's "seduction theory." Psychoanalysts have tended until recently to support the idea that women in psychoanalysis and psychotherapy who have reported being sexually abused by fathers and other male adults are, in most cases, reporting fantasies and not actual events. Initiated by Masson (1984) and reinforced by other researchers (Gediman, 1991), mental health professionals now tend to believe that the many women who report in their therapy that they have been sexually abused have, indeed, been so mistreated. Because of this shift in perspective, courts and ethics committees of professional organizations are now more apt to believe a woman who claims she was sexually abused by her therapist. Currently, about one-third of the states have made therapist-patient sexual relations illegal (Pope, 1986).

As the "seduction theory" has been questioned, the problem of incest has become another salient issue in the last two decades. Mental health workers have reported from their studies of caseloads in clinics and in other outpatient facilities a rate somewhere between 30% to 35% (Rosenfeld, 1979; Spencer, 1978). As the extremely disruptive and traumatic effects of incest have become more apparent (Gelinas, 1983; Strean, 1988), victims of sexual exploitation by their psychotherapists have been compared to victims of incest (Bates &

Brodsky, 1989). According to Barnhouse (1978), inasmuch as most, if not all, therapeutic relationships are characterized by the development of a powerful parent-child transference, sexual liaisons in therapy relationships are always "symbolically incestuous."

In his book, *Sexual Exploitation in Professional Relationships* (1989), Glen Gabbard points out:

> The analogy to incest is appropriate for a number of reasons. Incest victims and those who have been sexually exploited by professionals have remarkably similar symptoms: shame, intense guilt associated with a feeling that they were somehow responsible for their victimization, feelings of isolation and forced silence, poor self-esteem, suicidal and/or self-destructive behavior and denial. Reactions of friends and family—disbelief, discounting, embarrassment—are also similiar in both groups. (p. xi)

Concomitant with changes in the broader culture that have helped to focus more attention on sex between therapists and patients, there have been several new developments in the psychotherapy profession itself that make sex between clinician and patient a more pertinent topic.

Psychotherapists of the 1990s eschew the medical model that alleges that a healthy, mature, and wise professional treats an unhealthy, immature, and naive patient. Instead, most current mental health professionals avow that the therapeutic situation involves two imperfect, vulnerable human beings who form a partnership. Not only do the patient's transference reactions influence the process and outcome of the treatment, but the practitioner's subjective countertransference reactions make a major contribution as well (Fine, 1982; Kottler, 1986; Strean, 1990; Sussman, 1992). When patients and therapists accept with more assurance that therapists have definite responsibilities that influence the process and outcome of the treatment, the therapist will more likely be viewed as capable of behaving like the patient. Therefore, the therapist can also resist the therapeutic process in ways similar to the patient and demonstrate unresolved problems, such as the propensity to act out sexually. As the therapeutic situation has been more carefully researched, the person who becomes a psychotherapist has been more thoroughly investigated. For example, what attracts individuals to the practice of psychotherapy? It has been very well documented that many, if not most, psychotherapists have serious neurotic and interpersonal problems and in many cases suffer as much or more than their patients (Bermak, 1977; Burton, 1972; Deutsch, 1984; Finell, 1985; Freudenberger & Robbins, 1979; Maeder, 1989; Searles, 1975). Also, there is now a rich literature on countertransference difficulties that consistently suggests that countertransference is an ever-present phenomenon in psychotherapy (Brenner, 1985; Slakter, 1987; Teitelbaum, 1990); clinicians are much more willing to discuss their mistakes in the treatment situation, particularly how their characterological problems can inhibit and/or retard the therapeutic process (Baudry, 1991; Chused & Raphling, 1991).

In addition to the greater attention given to the therapeutic situation and to the psychodynamics of the mental health professional, more consideration has been given to the limitations and problems inherent in psychoanalytic and psychotherapeutic training programs, some of which may contribute to the sexual acting out of therapists with patients.

We will now turn to a detailed examination of the aforementioned phenomena that have made the issue of sexual liaisons between patient and therapist an important one both to professionals and to nonprofessionals. Let us begin our discussion with some of the more recent insights about the therapeutic situation.

THE THERAPEUTIC SITUATION

Sigmund Freud, the psychiatrist and neurologist from Vienna, is considered by most to be the founder of dynamic psychotherapy. Because Freud worked as a physician for many years, he tended to use a medical model to treat his patients. His early patients, as Freud assessed them, suffered from clear-cut illnesses, namely, anxiety neurosis, anxiety hysteria, and obsessive-compulsive neurosis. Those patients who could not be treated by his psychoanalytic method were afflicted by another illness, namely, schizophrenia (Freud, 1896).

Although there are still vestiges of the medical model observed in current psychotherapeutic practice, most mental health professionals have abandoned the paradigm of the sick patient who has to be treated for his illness by the authoritarian doctor. Patients and therapists tend to regard themselves as two vulnerable individuals who are quite similar in many ways, form an "alliance" (Greenson, 1967), and try to help the patient resolve conflicts so that he or she can enjoy working and loving with more freedom.

By the late 1950s, psychotherapists began to realize that each individual patient is unique and so complex that giving him or her a diagnostic label stereotypes the patient and fails to individualize him or her. In 1959, the highly respected psychiatrist and psychoanalyst Karl Menninger stated: "Diagnosis in the sense in which we doctors have used it for many years is not only relatively useless in many cases; it is an inaccurate, misleading, philosophically false predication" (1959, p. 672). In 1965, Anna Freud pointed out, "The descriptive nature of many current diagnostic categories runs counter to the essence of psychoanalytic thinking" (p. 110). As modern-day clinicians note, the standard psychological diagnostic system (the *Diagnostic and Statistical Manual of Mental Disorders* of the American Psychiatric Association) has proven to be so unsatisfactory in categorizing clinical phenomena that it has been repeatedly revised (Brill, 1965; Fine, 1982). Diagnostic systems do not describe the pain and anguish of someone who cannot love enthusiastically. They do not relate to the guilt that many patients feel in their day-to-day lives. They do not consider the anxiety that can be generated by aggressive and sexual fantasies that emerge in relationships. In sum, the medical model with its emphasis on diagnosis and treatment of an illness has been repudiated by most sophisticated professionals.

With the medical model essentially discarded, patients and therapists have begun to view each other very differently from the way they did in the early days of psychotherapy. The more democratic atmosphere in therapy with its emphasis on "relationship," "interaction," and "communication" has made the modal therapeutic situation much less sterile and more stimulating. Patients, instead of looking for treatment of illness, now seek an empathetic human being who will complement their own personalities and offer "corrective emotional experiences" and a "corrective emotional relationship" (Alexander, 1961).

Now that the therapeutic situation is more frequently conceptualized as one in which two human beings have intense feelings toward each other and mutually influence each other, countertransference is considered to be as crucial a dynamic variable in the therapeutic situation as transference. The same can be said about counterresistance and resistance (Strean, 1993). With the sharp focus on the human relationship in therapy, it has of course been inevitable that there would be much more appreciation by the therapist and patient of each other as sexual beings.

By the 1970s, clinicians became so preoccupied with the sexual dimension of the therapeutic situation that a few professionals began to openly advocate that sex be part of the therapeutic transaction in some cases. Martin Shepard (1971) in his book *The Love Treatment* took the position that the many women who needed to like themselves more as sexual beings and who seek psychotherapy would benefit by having sexual liaisons with their therapists. Feeling the emotional and sexual acceptance by their "love doctors" would help them accept themselves with more equanimity.

Around the time that Shepard was prescribing overt sex as part of "good" psychotherapy, Masters and Johnson (1970) were developing programs all over the country in which patients often had sex with their "sexual surrogates." Surrogates act as guides and mentors to those patients suffering from sexual difficulties. Much of the treatment involves surrogate and patient "pleasuring each other."

Somewhat similar to the Masters and Johnson program is Helen Kaplan's *The New Sex Therapy* (1974). Although not advocating "surrogates" as part of the treatment, her emphasis is on helping patients learn new sex techniques through active discussion and demonstration of helpful bodily exercises.

Concomitant with the "love treatments," "surrogate treatments," and the "new sex therapies" were the development of the encounter and sensitivity training movements. These "therapies" that very much influenced many therapists with differing theoretical perspectives prescribe touching, hugging, and "more physical interaction" between therapist and patient (Kovel, 1976).

By the late 1970s and early 1980s, the traditional therapeutic setting with its concentration on the "talking cure" was strongly challenged. The popularity of psychoanalysis, with its emphasis on introspection and not action, was declining. Group therapy and family therapy, with its emphasis on the "here and now," were on the ascendancy. The therapist was becoming much more of a "good friend" and much less of a dispassionate diagnostician and neutral therapist. Consequently, sex between patient and therapist was not such a foolhardy notion nor a remote possibility.

As historians have noted repeatedly, when there is a social or political movement going in one direction, there is often a countermovement (DeMause, 1981). This same phenomenon seems to occur in the mental health field as well. The emphasis on touching, hugging, and sexual contact that appeared to be gaining popularity in the early 1970s was met by opposition in the 1980s. Masters and Johnson began to have many critics (Fine, 1981; Karasu, Rosenbaum & Jerrett, 1979; Zilbergeld & Evans, 1980). The sensitivity and encounter movements were also seriously questioned (Kovel, 1976; Strean, 1976); writers like Shepard were reprimanded and repudiated (Bates & Brodsky, 1989). Many psychoanalysts and psychotherapists began to point out that the erotic transference was often "a bid for reassurance, a cover up for hostility, an expression of penis envy, an oral-incorporative wish, a defense against homosexuality, and all of these at different times" (Fine, 1982, p. 95). They also pointed out that many patients who talked about sex a great deal and made many sexual demands were often sexually starved and sexually conflicted (Karasu & Socarides, 1979).

During the 1980s and early 1990s, as dynamically oriented therapists and other mental health professionals began to speak out against overt sexual gratification in the therapy, lawsuits against therapists who transgressed became popular. Many books and articles pointed out that sex with the patient is similar to incest, rape, and other destructive acts (Bates & Brodsky, 1989; Freeman & Roy, 1976; Gabbard, 1989; Rutter, 1989). In this kind of atmosphere, it is understandable that few writers emerged who would speak with understanding about the severe disturbances in psychotherapists that led to their acting out sexually with patients. The therapist who acted out seemed to be more deserving of punishment than of humane treatment.

Although the tension was great between the traditional therapist who believed in a talking therapy with sexual abstinence and the one who championed physical contact, the controversy had some positive effects. Professionals like Masters and Johnson (1970), Helen Singer Kaplan (1974), and other behaviorists began to include in their programs some notions on transference, countertransference, and resistance. Dynamically oriented clinicians began to emphasize the importance of being more aware of the sexual dimension in therapy.

Stated Reuben Fine:

> Even though it is undesirable for therapists to act out attraction toward their patients, it is quite the opposite [to have] feelings. The more the therapist is able to experience a genuine liking for the patient, the more help he or she will be able to give. Because of the need to keep feelings in check, the analyst often takes the path of least

resistance, denying them altogether. This creates another problem for the patient, who in addition to feeling rejected for neurotic reasons is being rejected in reality. The fact that the therapist's rejection is a neurotic defense mechanism to protect him or her against his or her own sexual feelings does not alter the matter; in this way the analyst does not differ from other opposite-sex people whom the patient meets. (1982, p. 103)

Dr. Harold Searles averred that even with very emotionally disturbed women patients, it is crucial to give them the feeling that they are realistically attractive to the therapist. Said Searles:

Since I began doing psychoanalysis and intensive psychotherapy, I have found, time after time, that in the course of the work with every one of my patients who has progressed to, or very far towards, a thoroughgoing analytic cure, I have experienced romantic and erotic desires to marry, and fantasies of being married to, the patient. (1975, p. 284)

As the view of the therapeutic situation changed, so did notions on the patient who sought psychotherapy, particularly his or her similarities to and differences from the rest of the population.

CHANGING VIEWS OF THE
PATIENT IN PSYCHOTHERAPY

By the 1960s, many studies confirmed the presence of emotional conflicts in virtually every man, woman, and child (Dohrenwend & Dohrenwend, 1969; Leighton, 1963; Rennie, 1962); the difference between the patient diagnosed as "psychotic" and the so-called "normal" individual is only a matter of degree (Fine, 1990). As a result, more people from many diverse walks of life sought out mental health professionals for therapy. Social workers who traditionally worked with individuals of lower socioeconomic classes began to treat middle-class individuals and families, and psychoanalysts and psychiatrists who customarily worked with the more affluent began to treat individuals and families from lower socioeconomic classes (Henry, 1971). The realization that psychoanalysis and psychotherapy applied to all human beings had begun with Freud; the notion was becoming more of a truism by the mid-1960s.

As the patient began to be viewed less as a "sick person" and more as a troubled human being who was very similar to the clinician in many ways, therapist and patient gained more conviction that they had a great deal in common and grew much closer to each other. Furthermore, as the patient's conflicts were now being conceptualized as problems in loving and living, the therapist began to be considered more as an expert on love. Consequently, as love and sex emerged as dominant themes in therapeutic discourse, it became a common practice for therapists and patients to discuss the warm, loving, and sexual feelings that existed between them. Therefore, opportunities to act upon these feelings also became possible.

By the 1970s, many patients were perceived as individuals suffering from "deficits" rather than from neurotic symptoms only. These patients who experienced severe emotional deprivation in their early years needed, according to some experts, "parenting" rather than traditional treatment (Kohut, 1977). Thus, many mental health professionals rationalized their sexual contacts with these patients by pointing out that emotionally impoverished individuals needed the touch and embraces of the therapist who would be able to offer some restitution for the patient's deficits. This was, of course, Ferenczi's point of view propounded in the 1920s that reemerged fifty years later in rather popular form.

A much publicized case utilizing the aforementioned notions involved "the love treatment" of a medical student by a woman psychiatrist associated with Harvard University's medical school. Dr. Margaret Bean-Bayog sent notes to her patient, Paul

Lozano, such as, "I'm your mom and I love you and you love me very much. Say that 10 times." According to Bean-Bayog, this was her attempt to comfort an emotionally impoverished, deprived young man who needed the tender love and care from a mother figure. On the other hand, the lawyer for Lozano's family asserted that it was evidence that Bean-Bayog lured a brilliant young man into a morbid emotional and sexual relationship that left him deeply disturbed when she terminated it. A year after the end of therapy, Lozano died of a cocaine overdose—a death his parents believed was a suicide. Some 3,000 pages of notes and letters, tapes, books, and gifts exchanged by Lozano and Bean-Bayog were gathered by the Lozano family for a civil suit charging malpractice and wrongful death.

In an assessment of the documents, Adler and Rosenberg (1992) conclude:

> They depict a therapist so obsessed that she wrote to Lozano almost every day during her vacation. And they reveal a medical bureaucracy that took no action on another doctor's charge of "gross misconduct" against Bean-Bayog for more than a year, until the lawsuit brought the case into the headlines. . . . [Although] some psychiatric therapy entails "regression" in which the patient relives emotions from his childhood . . . the therapist is not supposed to direct and orchestrate this process, which is what Bean-Bayog seems to have done. Among the papers filed with the court are "flashcards" she prepared for him, bearing soothing evocations of childhood, such as these: "You too can act like a 3 year old when you're 25," says one. "You can curl up with a sweater, and the pound puppy (a stuffed animal toy) . . . and you can breastfeed and be cozy." Some were not so childlike: "I'm going to miss so many things about you . . . phenomenal sex and being so appreciated." (pp. 56–57)

The Bean-Bayog/Lozano case reflects what has dramatically transpired in the last two decades. Increasing numbers of patients have entered a greatly expanding arena of innovative "therapies." Many of these newer approaches have capitalized on sensationalism and promised substantial results in a brief period of time (Strupp, 1977). The magical wishes of many men and women in the expanded population of patients seeking therapeutic help have led them to consider sex with the clinician as a viable and quick cure.

Although "love treatments," with their emphasis on sexual contact between patient and therapist, have been publicized and analyzed more than ever before, it is important to keep in mind that as the number of individuals in psychotherapy has grown by leaps and bounds, the number of therapists and patients having sex is bound to increase. As sexual liaisons between therapists and patients have not only increased, but have been shown to seriously hurt many patients, a social movement among patients evolved during the last two decades. Hans Strupp, the eminent researcher of psychotherapy, has noted in his book *Psychotherapy for Better or Worse: The Problem of Negative Effects*:

> The emerging consumer advocacy movement has begun to influence the mental health field, with the result that many patients scrutinize with greater care the process and outcome of their therapy experience. In addition, consumer guides for selecting therapies and therapists, the move toward therapist-patient contracts, and lawsuits based on allegations of therapist malpractice all reflect increased consumer consciousness and thus a concern with the problem of negative effects in psychotherapy. (1977, p. 121)

With psychotherapy coming under a great deal of public scrutiny during the past two decades, patients have been more outspoken about their psychological and legal rights as patients (Freeman & Roy, 1976; Plasil, 1985). As a result, they have been trying to protect prospective patients, as well as those in treatment, from being sexually exploited and have stimulated psychotherapists to evaluate the type of patient who might be vulnerable to sexual manipulation by a therapist.

The patient of the 1990s realizes that the psychotherapy setting is an ideal milieu for extraordinary intimacy. Patient and therapist are isolated, "alone together," focusing on each other and feeling intense affects toward each other (Beck, 1992). Although some patients find the possibility of a close relationship with the therapist threatening and they either flee or fight, the majority, who have problems with love and loving, welcome the benign, warm, nonjudgmental atmosphere. But, some are at risk for having sex with the therapist.

Dr. Annette Brodsky (1989), who has done a great deal of research on sexual contacts between patients and therapists, has identified certain demographic and psychological characteristics of patients who are likely to be at risk of sexual exploitation. Such patients are most likely to be female. They do not enter treatment with complaints about their sexuality, but sexual difficulties are often suggested by the therapist. Wanting very much to trust the therapist, they accept his assessment. One major group of vulnerable patients is composed of those who have been physically or sexually abused as children. Some of them feel that this is the only way to relate to a parental figure (Strean, 1988).

The California Task Force Report of Sexual Intimacy (Bouhoutsos, 1983), which surveyed patients' second therapists, found that 30% of the patients had sex in the first few sessions with the first therapist. The sooner sexual contact between patient and therapist began, the shorter the period of time that therapy could be sustained.

Brodsky (1989) has also studied the consequences for patients who have had sexual contact with their therapists. They include suicidal feelings and increased use of drugs and alcohol. Other negative effects include worsening of sexual and marital relationships and mistrust of the opposite sex. In addition, patients were suspicious of future psychotherapists and refused to return for further help.

As interest in the type of individual who seeks out psychotherapy increased (Kadushin, 1969), and as research on the type of patient who is most vulnerable to sexual exploitation by therapists intensified, a corresponding interest evolved in therapists. During the past 20 years, there has been a burgeoning literature on the dynamics of those individuals who become psychotherapists and some research on the personal and professional characteristics of those mental health professionals who have sexual contact with their patients.

WHO BECOMES A PSYCHOTHERAPIST AND WHICH ONES ACT OUT SEXUALLY?

Although neglected until the 1980s, there is now a strong interest in the influence of the therapist's personality and dynamics on the therapeutic process. In the most intensive and extensive study on the subject, Dr. Michael Sussman (1992), in his book *A Curious Calling: Unconscious Motivations for Practicing Psychotherapy*, concludes that the psychological makeup of the individual psychotherapist determines, to a large extent, the effectiveness of the therapy.

In the 1970s, when I was teaching personality theory to doctoral candidates at Rutgers University, it occurred to the candidates and me that the major constructs of each personality theory that we studied emanated from the story of the theorist's life. For example, Alfred Adler, who was physically ill as a young boy and extremely jealous of his older brother, suggested that the bases of neuroses were the patient's subjective states of "organic inferiority" and his or her "ordinal position in the family." Karen Horney, who posited the notion that the neurotic personality "feels lonely in a hostile world," was the daughter of a seaman who was frequently absent from home. Harry Stack Sullivan believed that every child, in order to mature, needed "a chum"; as a young boy Sullivan was a friendless fellow living in social isolation on a farm. The framer of the "oedipus complex," Sigmund Freud, as a youngster slept in the parental bedroom (Strean, 1975).

Around the time that the doctoral candidates and I were examining some of the personality dynamics of theorists, I learned that two colleagues of mine in another department at Rutgers had been doing intensive and extensive research on the subject. In their book *Faces in a Cloud: Subjectivity in Personality Theory* (1979), Drs. Robert Stolorow and George Atwood performed an invaluable service with their pioneering work. They demonstrate in rich detail how Otto Rank's notions on "birth trauma" and "separation anxiety" are very much linked to his subjective view of his own "horrible birth" and to continual problems that he experienced in interpersonal relationships — always unable to sustain a relationship, yet miserable when he was separated from someone. Stolorow and Atwood also show how Jung's "collective unconscious" emanates from his rigid religious background that caused him to feel very alienated from the rest of the world. In addition, the authors demonstrate how Wilhelm Reich's construct of "character armor" is related to his paranoid view of the world.

It is now well accepted among psychotherapists that the theoretical perspective that clinicians endorse, the modality of therapy that they favor, and the patients with whom therapists do well or poorly in treatment are very much related to the stories of the clinicians' lives and their psychodynamics, with both their conflict-free spheres and their neurotic propensities. Since the late 1970s, two major shifts in focus have manifested themselves in the professional literature. There is now a rich literature on countertransference and, related to this shift, several clinicians have written books offering personal accounts of their experiences as psychotherapists.

In 1910 when Freud first wrote on the subject of counter-transference, he said:

> We have become aware of "the counter-transference" which arises [in the analyst] as a result of the patient's influence on his unconscious feelings, and we are almost inclined to insist that he shall recognize this counter-transference in himself and overcome it. . . .We have

noticed that no psycho-analyst goes further than his own complexes and internal resistances permit. (pp. 144–145)

Although Freud's statement of over 80 years ago—that the therapist can help the patient mature only to the point that the therapist himself or herself has travelled—is as valid today as it was in 1910, Freud's original idea that countertransference means unconscious interference with a therapist's ability to understand patients has been considerably broadened. Sander Abend (1989) points out in his paper "Countertransference and Psychoanalytic Technique": "Current usage [of the term countertransference] often includes all of the emotional reactions of the analyst at work" (p. 374). Slakter (1987) defines "countertransference" as "all those reactions of the analyst to the patient that may help or hinder treatment" (p. 3).

It is interesting to note that as countertransference has been viewed as more of a crucial variable in treatment by most therapists, the major contributions to the expanded definition have come from the more conservative Freudian psychoanalysts. For example, Joseph Sandler (1976) has pointed out how therapists unconsciously respond to patients' needs for them to be and act a certain way, a phenomenon for which he suggests the term "role responsiveness." Blum (1986) has discussed some of the irrational reactions on the part of therapists to the work of psychotherapy and psychoanalysis as well as to the impact that events in the clinician's life may have on the countertransference. Abend (1982) has written of the effect of the clinician's illness on the countertransference.

In joining the many clinicians who strongly believe that psychotherapy is an interactional process, Boesky (1990) said: "If there can be no [psychotherapy] without resistance by the patient, then it is equally true that there can be no treatment conducted by any [therapist] without counterresistance or countertransference, sooner or later" (p. 573). Baranger (1983) in a similar vein said, "He who doesn't cry doesn't get cured... and he who doesn't cry doesn't cure" (p. 10).

As the therapeutic process has been more intensively studied during the past two decades, it has been acknowledged that therapists, like patients, frequently find themselves getting emotionally involved in ways they have not intended (Boesky, 1990). In other words, both the patient and the therapist have similar propensities to regress, act out, and become infantile.

Two major consequences have emerged from recognizing that psychotherapy is definitely an interactional process with countertransference contributions being as crucial as transference reactions. The first consequence, and the most positive, is that psychotherapists are taking much more responsibility for their own contributions to therapeutic stalemates and to other forms of therapeutic failure (Weinshel, 1990). No longer is the success or failure of the psychotherapeutic process attributable to the patient alone.

With countertransference now considered to be an inevitable part of the therapeutic interaction, some clinicians have allowed themselves more spontaneity in the clinical situation—often making self-disclosures and verbalizing their own feelings toward the patient (Searles, 1979). This second consequence has, of course, prompted some clinicians to share their sexual fantasies toward the patient with the patient and then move toward having sexual contact (Walker & Young, 1986). In effect, one of the unanticipated consequences of the move toward appreciating and discussing psychotherapy as an interactional process has stimulated some therapists to interact sexually with their patients (Bates & Brodsky, 1989; Freeman & Roy, 1976; Gabbard, 1989), a move that usually, if not always, has negative effects on both.

In the last two decades, there have been several books published that reveal just what the therapist experiences internally as he or she works with his or her patients, particularly how the story of the therapist's life affects the interactional process. In this regard, it should be mentioned that Freud's inner world has been revealed more with the passage of time. Ernest Jones's (1957) biographical work on Freud has been complemented and supplemented by a host of other biographers (Anzieu, 1986; Clark, 1980; Gay, 1988; Grinstein, 1980; Masson, 1985; Sulloway,

1979). Since the mid-1980s the personal lives of therapists are actively discussed (Goldberg, 1986; Kottler, 1986; Strean, 1990; Sussman, 1992).

Sussman's (1992) extensive research on the unconscious motivations for practicing psychotherapy concludes that "behind the wish to practice psychotherapy lies the need to cure one's inner wounds and unresolved conflicts" (p. 19). His conclusion has been reaffirmed by many other researchers; Guy and Liaboe (1985) have demonstrated that therapists commit suicide at a rate that exceeds that of the general population, and Moore (1982) in her study reported that female psychiatrists commit suicide at a rate 47 times that of the general population. Bermak (1977) found that more than 90% of the therapists that he studied experienced a wide variety of serious mental disturbances.

Very often it is alleged that the therapist's own therapy or personal analysis equips him or her to be less vulnerable to countertransference difficulties and less prone to emotional disturbances. Although this is probably true to some extent, as early as 1947, one of the leading psychotherapists and psychoanalysts made a statement that is as true today as it was almost half a century ago:

> Psychoneurotic trends in our present state of civilization are so universal that a person who is practically free of them or their equivalents is a rare exception, still less likely to be found among those who want to become analysts because the vivid interest in the psychoneuroses, their etiology and therapy, is regularly motivated by one's own neurotic problems, past or present, and more often the latter. (Sachs, 1947, p. 158)

In 1976 Shapiro, in a study of over 100 graduates of the Columbia University Psychoanalytic Center for Training and Research, pointed out:

> Considering the special motivations of persons attracted to psychoanalysis as a life work, the relatively high percentage

of personal pathology acknowledged by this group reflects
the degree to which pain, suffering, conflict, and the wish
to understand and master them can prompt a sustained,
even life-long, interest in introspection, understanding,
and resolution of conflict. (p. 20)

Not only has it been realized that those who choose to enter
the mental health professions typically manifest significant
psychopathology of their own (Sussman, 1992), but also there
has been some investigation regarding the nature of the pathology that therapists bring into the treatment situation.

A number of writers have pointed to the unconscious voy-
eurism that many therapists attempt to gratify in their work.
Doing therapy requires looking beneath the surface and
learning about many "forbidden" issues (Greenson, 1967;
Menninger, 1957; Sussman, 1992); many clinicians do attempt
to "help" their patients talk about taboo subjects under the guise
of liberating them (Serban, 1981).

Being privy to the sexual life of patients and becoming the
object of patients' erotic desires can offer much stimulation and
reassurance to the many "wounded healers" who are in the
mental health professions (Sussman, 1992). The temptation
induced in the psychotherapist to accede to the patient's desires
for sex and/or to initiate sexual contact with the patient was an
issue that preoccupied Freud and has been a concern of most
of the leading clinicians to this day. In his paper, "Observations
on Transference Love," Freud (1915) wrote in part:

For the physician there are ethical motives which combine
with the technical reasons to hinder him from according
the patient his love. The aim that he has to keep in view
is that this woman, whose capacity for love is disabled by
infantile fixations, should attain complete access over this
function which is so inestimably important for her in life,
not that she should fritter it away in the treatment, but
preserve it for real life, if so be that after her cure, life
makes that demand on her. . . .

However highly [the therapist] may prize love, he must prize even more highly the opportunity to help his patient over a decisive moment in her life. . . .

The analytic psychotherapist thus has a threefold battle to wage—in his own mind against the forces which would draw him below the level of analysis; outside analysis against the opponents who dispute the importance he attaches to the sexual instinctual forces and hinder him from making use of them in his scientific method; and in the analysis against his patients, who at first behave like his critics but later on disclose the overestimation of sexual life which has them in thrall, and who try to take him captive in the net of their socially ungovernable passions. (pp. 169–170)

Almost 70 years after Freud wrote his paper on transference love, Reuben Fine (1982) in *The Healing of the Mind* reiterated Freud's admonitions and in commenting on sexual desires in the therapist, he said:

Gratifying the sexual wish [of the patient] has several consequences. First, it turns the analysis into a love affair, thereby negating its long-term benefits, even if the short-term gains are sweeter. And second, as a love affair the analysis is not different from any other love affair—offering temporary pleasure but no deep inner change. It is also worth remembering that while the analyst may be well trained professionally, there is no guarantee that he or she is equally well trained as a lover. A third consequence is even more serious. As in any love affair, sooner or later one party, usually the woman, will probably push for marriage. If the analyst refuses, the woman will feel doubly rejected, first because her lover has turned her down and second, because her analyst has found her unworthy of marriage. The results of this double rejection can be calamitous. (pp. 101-102)

These caveats, Fine's virtually identical to those of Freud's, have been repeated many times by many writers over many decades. Yet, 10% to 20% of mental health professionals find it difficult to heed these warnings (Gabbard, 1989; Pope, 1986).

It has been acknowledged by most clinicians that the nature of the therapeutic relationship is a very intimate one, a relationship that has been termed "a quasi-courtship" (Scheflen, 1965). In this intimate courtship, there are often many forms of covert seduction taking place between the therapy partners. As they try to mutually influence each other, they can use such devices as flattery, sympathy, and other types of inviting communications (Edelwich & Brodsky, 1991). How often covert seduction occurs in therapy is difficult to know and has not been researched very much. However, as mentioned, overt sexuality between therapist and patient has been reported with more regularity in the last two decades.

Let us now review some of the research on overt sexuality between patient and therapist, and in consonance with our focus, specifically the literature that deals principally with the therapist's role in the sexual liaison and on the clinician's fantasies, conflicts, and attitudes toward the patient.

REVIEW OF THE LITERATURE ON THE THERAPIST'S ROLE IN SEXUAL LIAISONS WITH PATIENTS

According to Brodsky (1989), in the 1950s and 1960s some mental health professionals collected data on sex between therapists and patients, but they feared the idea of presenting the data formally. Although the topic appeared too controversial to present at conferences or to publish in journals and books until the 1970s, there were some references to the subject prior to the 1970s.

Marmor (1953) discussed the feeling of superiority that is frequently induced in clinicians by many of their patients. The grandiosity and omnipotence can intensify during the course of doing therapeutic work and can lead the clinician to the narcissistic conviction that his superior personality with its magical libido can cure the patient! Infantile narcissism, as first noted by Marmor, has been observed by many writers. Claman (1987) concluded that a narcissistic disturbance is at the root of many therapists who have sex with their patients. Twemlow and Gabbard (1989) in their paper "The Lovesick Therapist" report the same finding as does Smith (1989) in his work, "The Seduction of the Female Patient." Twemlow and Gabbard (1989) point out that narcissistic problems are "often overlooked in the therapist's personal analysis or therapy, and the practice of psychotherapy itself provides a number of narcissistic gratifications. The therapist who needs to be loved and idealized can always find patients who will fulfill that need" (p. 80). Finell (1985), Miller (1981), and Sussman (1992) have all suggested that those who enter the field of psychotherapy have narcissistic disturbances.

In 1966, James McCartney wrote about "overt transference" as a tangible, muscular, glandular response to a highly subjective inner feeling that represents a need to do "more than talk." He received the consent from 1500 women and their families who "needed to do more than talk" to include sex in the treatment. As one reads McCartney's material it would appear that he himself needed to do more than talk.

By the late 1960s and early 1970s, we can find a few writers prescribing sexual gratification as a legitimate form of psychotherapy. In addition to McCartney (1966), who felt that patients "need" to caress, fondle, examine his body, and engage in intercourse with him from time to time, Elizabeth Mintz (1969) suggested that therapists touch their patients, embrace them, and fondle them in order to lower resistances and gratify childish wishes that were frustrated by their patients' parents. Shepard (1971), to whom we referred earlier, interviewed several patients who had sex with therapists. Although he claimed that the sex had therapeutic benefits, his clinical data do not easily substantiate these claims. Dahlberg (1970) in his paper on sexual contacts between patients and therapists was one of the first to hypothesize about the dynamics of the therapist who has sex with his patients. His major conclusion was that the therapists were aging men going through a depressed period who let themselves be convinced by their patients' fantasies that they, the therapists, might recapture a lost or fantasied youth. The narcissistic enrichment that the sex provided these therapists seemed quite apparent. Dahlberg also reported that he had been trying without success to publish his data for many years. Most editors that he consulted took the position that his case material was too controversial.

In 1970 Masters and Johnson published *Human Sexual Inadequacy*. In their evaluation of women patients who had sex with their previous therapists, Masters and Johnson recommended strict sanctions against such therapists and they themselves stopped using sex surrogates to aid patients in overcoming sexual inhibitions. At this time therapists were starting to acknowledge openly their own sexual gratifications in doing therapy. Marmor (1972) introduced the concept of "countertransference sexual acting out," pointing out that the therapists could be equally as seductive as the patient in their interactions in the therapeutic encounter.

Although many individuals, therapists and nontherapists, had recognized and accepted that patients yearn for sexual contact with the clinician in order to gratify intense incestuous and oedipal fantasies, around the mid-1970s writers began to suggest that therapists could just as easily unconsciously turn patients into parental figures. In so doing, a sexual contact with the patient by a clinician could be an attempt on the therapist's part to gratify his or her own forbidden and intense incestuous and oedipal fantasies (Kardener, 1974; Sussman, 1992).

Those who have considered some of the unconscious motivations in therapists who have sex with their patients agree that these therapists are frequently trying to cope with, and usually are trying to deny, strong homosexual fantasies in themselves. For example, in the case of the promiscuous male therapist who suffers from the "Don Juan syndrome" (Marmor, 1976), this individual can repress his wishes to be a sexual woman and work overtime to be a sexual "he-man." He does not recognize that beneath his compulsive sexuality is a strong identification with his women patients (Twemlow & Gabbard, 1989).

Very often therapists who have problems with their sexual identities begin to question their competence as professionals. Exploitation of a positive transference by having sex enables these therapists to receive narcissistic supplies that are missing from their daily lives (Butler & Zelen, 1977) and to calm their self-doubts temporarily (Gabbard, 1989).

In the 1980s there were over 100 cases of therapist-patient sexual liaisons brought to ethics committees of licensing boards in the mental health professions (Brodsky, 1989). Also at this time, researchers began to reflect much more on the nature of the sex between therapists and patients. Wishes to rape, to gratify incestuous wishes and oedipal desires, to overcome depression, and to defend against homosexuality were often seen as the most prominent motives by many researchers (Gabbard, 1989; Smith, 1989; Sussman, 1992). Apfel and Simon (1986) insightfully suggested that some clinicians who felt very depressed may engage in sexual intimacies with their patients in order to get caught by colleagues. This would gratify wishes for all kinds of real and imagined transgressions and also could serve as a disguised cry for the therapeutic help they so much want and need. Smith (1989) made the same observation.

Desperate therapists described by Apfel and Simon (1986) and Smith (1989) may be likened to those clinicians who were described by Searles (1979). These clinicians, it appeared, became involved in sexual intimacies with their patients because they could not reach their patients in any other way. If they could not "penetrate" their patients with verbal interventions, they seemed to have decided that they could derive more "therapeutic" success with their penises.

In an insightful paper, "Countertransference Reactions to the Difficult Patient," Reuben Fine (1984) discussed some of his observations and impressions of therapists who had been involved sexually with their patients. He stated: "In all these cases the therapist displayed different dynamic patterns, so that the sex could not be explained in any uniformly simplistic way: one was frightened, another was sadistic, a third was confused, a fourth [was defending against] homosexuality" (p. 20). In his paper, Fine refers to Dahlberg's research (1970) cited earlier in this chapter. Fine felt that Dahlberg's conclusion that the sexually acting-out therapists were ordinary aging men in a depressive mood trying to recapture a lost youth was "oversimplistic." Fine pointed out that sex with the patient serves a purpose in the therapist's psychic life. According to Fine, often the therapist is teasing the woman in order to seek revenge against the women in his life whom he feels have hurt him. The therapists were giving the women patients sex and then abandoning them—something similar to the way they felt when they were sadistically treated.

Along with attempts to study the psychodynamics of therapists who have sex with their patients were more revelations— revelations of well-known clinicians having sex. In his book, *Final Analysis,* Jeffrey Masson (1990) quotes the internationally renowned psychoanalyst Masud Khan as saying, "I never sleep with other analysts' patients, only my own" (p. 161). Masson also reports that Masud Khan was not only living with a former patient, but continued to see her husband in analysis. Masson also quotes the well-known analyst, Muriel Gardner, who said to Masson, ". . .the way I see most analysts behave in the every-day world simply appalls me. I know it appalls Anna Freud too, because we've talked about it plenty. I can't tell you how many analysts come to confess sleeping with patients" (p. 186).

In his extensive research on "The Seduction of the Female Patient," Smith (1989) points out that the therapist who feels very vulnerable and unable to cope with his own psychological problems often confides his personal problems to the patient. This may then arouse the patient to find ways to comfort the therapist, and this comfort can be quickly turned into sexual acts. Turning the patient into a quasi-therapist rather than going to his own therapist for help has been observed by many authors (Bates & Brodsky, 1989; Brodsky, 1989; Gabbard, 1989; Rutter, 1989). By so doing, the therapist is not only abdicating his own responsibility as a therapist, but by moving the "conversations" into sex, he seems to be tacitly devaluing psychotherapy as a helping process.

In his research, Smith (1989) points out that when one hears about the therapist seducing the patient, it is fairly easy to infer that there is not a loving relationship taking place, but usually there is a great deal of aggressive acting out on the part of the therapist. Certainly the sadistic quality of the therapist was well documented in *Sex in the Therapy Hour: A Case of Professional Incest* (Bates & Brodsky, 1989) and in *Betrayal* (Freeman & Roy, 1976). Fine (1984), Gabbard (1989), and Sussman (1992) have all referred to the sadism in the sexually acting-out therapist.

As referred to previously, Twemlow and Gabbard (1989) describe "The Lovesick Therapist." This is a professional who believes he has fallen in love with his patient and cannot think of anybody or anything else other than his adored patient. He has strong physical reactions when thinking of his "loved one," his heart goes "bumpity bump," and he feels he is "walking on air." In looking at the dynamics of this therapist, Twemlow and Gabbard note that there is a strong infantile quality to him. The personal and sexual involvement with his patient in many ways is reminiscent of a baby in his mother's arms or at her breast. It would appear that "the lovesick therapist" has regressed to a symbiotic state and has psychologically merged with his "mother-patient." The attraction between patient and therapist seems to be a narcissistic one in which both partners feel like ecstatic and blissful infants who have found nirvana.

Although having sex with a patient has been defined as an "illegal" and "unethical" act, few researchers have found therapists who seduce their patients to be psychopathic (Gabbard, 1989). Rather, as Smith (1989) and Apfel and Simon (1986) have noted, many of these professionals seem to be asking for punishment. In many ways they could be described as "Criminals Out of a Sense of Guilt" (Freud, 1916), individuals who want to be punished for acts or unconscious fantasies that activate guilt.

Peter Rutter (1989) in a popular book called *Sex in the Forbidden*

Zone, after finding himself close to a sexual involvement with a female patient, writes of the latent potential for this in all mental health professionals and says that "sexual exploitation of professional relationships is epidemic in our society" (p. 15). His research yielded the fact that "96 percent (a consensus figure based on studies that have been done) of sexual exploitation by professionals occurs between a man in power and a woman under his care" (p. 22). Of course, most statistical studies are unreliable because they rely on the few therapists who are willing to admit to their sexual involvements with patients. Rutter seems to have recognized this. In fact, he points out that "the dearth of literature or articles that existed on sexual exploitation in the professions in 1984, when my research began, was shocking" (p. 36).

Like many others (Gabbard, 1989; Marmor, 1976; Sussman, 1992), Rutter views the clinician who has sex with patients as a "wounded healer" who is trying to restore himself from a feeling of incompleteness to one of wholeness. It would appear that just as the patient who feels injured and needs care can fall in love with a therapist and want to have sex, the therapist who engages in sex with his patient feels just as wounded and just as needy. As Rutter states: "Clearly, the men who are the healers in forbidden-zone relationships often have as much a need to be healed through them as do their protegees" (p. 66). Describing a colleague, a respected, successful psychiatrist, who disclosed to Rutter that he had an affair with a patient, the colleague was "unable to resist the magical healing opportunity that he was sure sexual contact with her would provide" (p. 66).

One of Freud's statements regarding sexual acting out by the therapist comes from his paper on transference love (1915). Freud commented:

> [The analyst] must recognize that the patient's falling in love is induced by the analytic situation and is not to be attributed to the charms of his own person; so that he has no grounds whatever for being proud of such a "conquest," as it would be called outside analysis. (pp. 160–161)

Every therapist who has sex with a patient has mistaken the transference as real. However, as Andrea Celenza (1991) points out, the therapist has also misunderstood his own countertransference love and experiences it as "the real thing." Although every love relationship has components of transference, it is the therapist's job to help himself and the patient understand transference wishes, not gratify them. Celenza, in her paper "The Misuse of Countertransference Love in Sexual Intimacies Between Therapists and Patients" quotes the late and eminent psychoanalyst Elvin Semrad, who is remembered to have said to an adoring female patient: "You feel this way for neurotic reasons and when you get better, I will be very sad" (pp. 501–502). Just as Frayn and Silberfeld (1986) note that an eroticized transference is "a demand for love in the absence of a capacity for loving" (p. 323), the same can be said about an eroticized countertransference.

Just as the patients who are likely to have sex with their therapists have been identified by certain psychological and demographic characteristics, therapists can be similarly identified. Brodsky (1989) points out what other researchers have consistently reported: the therapist involved in sexual intimacy with patients is usually a male. Although there have been female therapists identified as transgressors, most often their affairs have been with lesbian patients and they represent a small proportion of the population of clinicians having sex with patients. Extremely few male-male dyads have been reported.

The modal therapist involved sexually with his patients is a middle-aged man and is typically about 15 years older than the patient. Usually this therapist is very unhappy with his own love relationships, has a poor marriage and/or may be going through a divorce proceeding. Although he has experienced a great deal of conflict in his interpersonal relationships with women, he tends to see predominantly women patients in his practice. He is likely to be involved sexually with more than one patient at a time (Brodsky, 1989; Gabbard, 1989; Sussman, 1992).

The therapist who forms sexual liaisons with his patients tends to be a professional who behaves in many antitherapeutic ways. He has patients work for him, advise him in real estate or finance and may even socialize with them (Brodsky, 1989). As has been pointed out a few times in this chapter, clinicians who become sexually involved with their patients tend to disclose features of their personal lives to their patients, particularly areas of interpersonal conflict (Twemlow & Gabbard, 1989).

Another characteristic of the sexualizing practitioner is that he tends to be an isolated professional (Brodsky, 1989). Even if he works in a clinic or an agency, he does not consult very much with his peers—perhaps because he is worried about being discovered. Although he does not come off as a very sensitive or competent sexual partner (Bates & Brodsky, 1989; Freeman & Roy, 1976; Plasil, 1985), the therapist is idealized and loved for long periods of time by the women patients with whom he has sex.

THE TRAINING OF THE PSYCHOTHERAPIST AND ITS IMPACT ON SEXUAL ACTING OUT

Some consideration should be given to the training programs of psychotherapists and how they might contribute to sexual acting out.

Earlier in this chapter it was recalled that many esteemed members of Freud's inner circle, Jung, Ferenczi, Rank, and Jones, were all reported to have sexual contacts with their patients. Perhaps some of the dynamics inherent in Freud's inner circle have continued to be expressed in other training circles?

One of the most obvious features of psychotherapeutic training is that teachers, supervisors, training analysts, and training therapists are idealized while students, supervisees, and clinicians in treatment are infantilized. Just as Freud tended to foster a father-son interaction with his followers, trainers of therapists tend to do the same. Arlow (1972) suggests that the typical psychoanalytic training program fosters a great deal of childish dependency in candidates; consequently, they often find it difficult to think for themselves and cannot feel too autonomous or experience much self-esteem. Jaques (1976) refers to the "paranoigenic" atmosphere of psychotherapeutic training institutes where idealization of parental figures is encouraged and, as a result, candidates worry about being "persecuted." Kernberg (1986) poignantly and comprehensively discusses how the personal therapy of trainees is corrupted because of "an illness affecting the educational structures of psychoanalytic institutes and societies" (p. 799). This illness involves sadistic treatment of candidates, characterized by frequent teasing and taunting of them, and a constant stimulation of many unrealizable childish fantasies.

When therapists are trained in institutions where traditional therapeutic barriers are crossed, that is, when they see their own analysts and therapists in all kinds of extratherapeutic situations (classrooms, meetings, social events), there is, of course, going to be a tendency on their part to cross barriers with their own psychological sons and daughters, that is, their patients. Furthermore, when therapists as patients receive constant indulgences and transference gratifications, their yearning to be the analyst's or therapist's favorite child is constantly being kindled and rekindled. To cope with their wishes to be their mentor's favorite child and have a special relationship with him or her, the therapist can do what many frustrated parents do—live vicariously through their own children and give to them what they desperately wanted but never achieved. It seems quite clear that many clinicians who turn therapy with their patients into love affairs are providing their patients with what they yearned for—a love affair with their own analyst or therapist.

In a paper, "The New York Psychoanalytic Civil War," Frosch (1991) thoroughly documents how the psychotherapeutic world, ever since its inception, has been characterized by factions, splits, and dissensions. When psychoanalytic institutes and other training centers are seats of conflict with much hatred visible, candidates, like children in a family, are going to feel inclined to rebel against the family's traditional values. One way of discharging contempt toward one's "psychotherapy family" is by violating its manifest code of conduct and having affairs with patients.

In the paper mentioned above, Frosch points out that therapists and analysts in training consistently observe dissensions and schisms in their institutes that are frequently reminiscent of the tensions they experienced in their own homes. Frosch writes:

> According to some (Eckardt, Horney's daughter, 1978), the quarreling and splitting that occurred at the American Academy of Psychoanalysis was a reenactment on a larger scale of the quarreling of the young Karen's parents throughout her childhood. Just as she had never found much peace at home, Karen Horney was never able to create a tranquil cooperative atmosphere in the organization she founded. (1991, p. 1051)

The "culture" of the therapist's training facility is an integral factor in shaping his or her attitudes toward patients. When boundaries are consistently crossed, when sadism and masochism are constantly being expressed, when strong wishes for narcissistic satisfaction are frequently being stimulated, the possibilities for sexual acting out by therapists are increased. It should be mentioned here that therapists are not trained in any formal way not to act out sexually. It is something that is just assumed, much like priests are not formally trained to be celibate. It is taken for granted by their mentors that they will abstain sexually, but like therapists, they, too, are known to have sexual contacts with their clientele.

The therapy culture, of course, is very much part of the web of the societal culture. Let us now turn to a discussion of how trends in society can influence the role of the therapist, particularly his or her sexual behavior with patients.

SOCIETY AND THE PSYCHOTHERAPIST

Rapid social change has been one of the most apparent features of our twentieth century culture. Americans have been described as suffering from severe disorientation and inability to cope with the many stresses sparked by the continual flow of cultural change in contemporary society (Packard, 1968; Strean, 1980; Toffler, 1970). Perhaps the most notable shift in interpersonal relationships has been the interaction between men and women. Today more than half of all married women work outside the home. As they move into parts of the economic orbit traditionally restricted to men, contemporary women are actively competing with men and are repudiating their formerly subordinate roles.

Rather than submit to the authority of their husbands in most matters, married women in our society are attempting to expand their personal horizons. Some groups in the women's movement have argued that a woman who commits herself to one man is collaborating in her own oppression (Durbin, 1977) and that traditional marriage is a form of serfdom or slavery (Smith & Smith, 1974). It has been estimated that over 50% of married people are having extramarital affairs (Felton, 1984; Richardson, 1985; Strean, 1980) and millions are "swinging" and "switching." As early as 1964 it was estimated that as many as 8 million couples had participated in the practice of exchanging partners for sexual purposes (Breedlove & Breedlove, 1964).

As men and women take on new role-sets, and as privileges, pleasures, and responsibilities assigned exclusively to one gender are being reconsidered, tensions between husbands and wives as well as between men and women in general are probably higher than ever before in our society. One indication of this tension is the fact that there is now over one divorce for every two marriages in the United States (Fincham & Bradbury, 1990). Marriage has become a chancy, grim, modern experiment instead of an ancient institution (Howard, 1978).

We now live in a psychologically sophisticated era that puts much emphasis on the right of the individual to personal emotional satisfaction and fulfillment. A public, widely disillusioned by wars, scandals, and unstable societal institutions, shares the belief that good times should be sought in the here and now (Williamson, 1977). Today's husband and wife are constantly being stimulated by the lure of many potential pleasures. Eroticism in both advertisements and the popular media is flooding the market, promising increased happiness, self-esteem, and joy to those who heed the message. For over two decades we have been "swirling in the vortex of the sexual sell, which has led many into believing that any behavior in which they wish to indulge is permissible under the banner of sexual freedom" (Spotnitz & Freeman, 1964, p. 21).

During the last two decades, many individuals have been led to believe that life can be ecstatic and that one can be loved, adored, and admired most of the time, provided that one learns the right methods to achieve the promised state of bliss. Self-help books insist that happiness is to be achieved by self-aggrandizement and fulfillment of narcissistic fantasies. Many people today are experiencing a decline in the strength of the superego; guilt seems to be less regarded as an appropriate response to egocentric behavior (Strean, 1980). In the popular film, *An Unmarried Woman*, when the distraught wife tells her therapist that she feels very guilty because she believes she provoked her husband to leave her for another woman, the therapist orders her to "take a rest from guilt!" – choosing not to help her patient with the anger and other feelings and fantasies that contributed to her guilt.

Our "age of sensation" (Hendin, 1975) has certainly influenced most if not all of the members of the mental health professions. It has been determined that many psychotherapists have claimed during the last two decades that nothing one does or does not do should be considered wrong or immoral unless it gets him or her in trouble (Strean, 1976; Strean, 1980). Many therapists have tended to renounce Freud's prescription for healthy mental life, which is "to love and to work" but in a monitored and disciplined manner. The emphasis now is not on "Where there is id, there shall be ego"; rather, many therapists have joined those in our culture who are actively rebelling against restraints and are really proclaiming, "Where there is ego, there shall be id."

Many of the newer therapies that have emerged in the last two decades—the encounter groups, nude marathons, sensitivity groups, and some group therapies—reflect our hedonistic society's dominant values with its emphasis on instant gratification. In paralleling the quest for the "quick fix" that exists in our culture, the newer and popular therapies are advertised in a manner that is similar to the advertisements of cold creams. A come-on such as "12 sessions of an encounter group will make you the attractive person you want to be" caters to the patient's narcissism, activates grandiose fantasies, and increases sexual tension.

Now that instant gratification and narcissistic satisfaction are emphasized in therapy, the role of the therapist has been much modified. The current social order wants the therapist to alter his or her stance; instead of helping patients achieve self-understanding, cope with frustration, and accept others with more equanimity, the contemporary clinician should not only be an advocate of id pleasure, but is often expected to participate in it right in the therapy! Proof of this shift are the many movies that turn the therapist into a sexual partner of the patient's (Gabbard & Gabbard, 1987).

In the film *Lovesick*, Dudley Moore plays the role of a therapist who is smitten by his beautiful patient. When Moore is advised by his colleagues to stop his affair, his colleagues appear to be uptight morons and the audience enjoys Moore's decision to defy professional norms. In *Prince of Tides*, Barbra Streisand, a woman psychoanalyst, has an affair with the twin brother of her female patient and the audience enjoys Streisand's spontaneity and unrestrained eroticism with her patient's brother. In *Final Analysis*, Richard Gere is a San Francisco psychiatrist who quickly overcomes any ethical quibbles he has about sleeping with a patient's sister. Sexual intimacies between patient and therapist also take place in *Dressed to Kill*, *Zelig*, and

House of Games. And in the play *Jake's Women,* Alan Alda is told by his female therapist that if he falls in love with her, he will be cured. Current biographies and television also depict the therapist as a lover with his patient. In a popular biography of Anne Sexton, the renowned poet, Sexton and one of her therapists become lovers (Sexton & Ames, 1991). A television program that created much interest in 1992 was "My Doctor, My Lover," in which the program *Frontline* depicted a real love affair between a psychiatrist and his patient. Although the patient suffered greatly from the sexual exploitation by the psychiatrist, Dr. Richter, the psychiatrist was exonerated by the courts and continued to practice psychotherapy.

When the therapist is frequently portrayed as a lover in the cinema and elsewhere, when instant gratification becomes very much endorsed by many mental health professionals, when affairs and one-night stands are more acceptable by the married and unmarried, when the institution of marriage is very unstable, then all of these social variables provide both stimulation and reinforcement for the therapist to consider having sex with a patient and to rationalize it as a sound therapeutic procedure.

It should be mentioned that other professionals in additon to those in the mental health field have been affected by the society's changing mores. Sipe (1990), a former priest, in his book *A Secret World: Sexuality and the Search for Celibacy,* writes about members of the clergy who have sexual affairs with their congregants, and in *Sex in the Forbidden Zone,* Rutter (1989) reports that many lawyers, physicians, and teachers are having sexual relationships with their clientele.

Despite the AIDS epidemic, the majority of men and women in our society, married and unmarried, professionals and nonprofessionals, have more than one sexual partner. This seems to be true of many mental health professionals as well. According to Gabbard (1991), "Many therapists may pay far more attention to their patients than to their spouses. Therapists who link their gratification exclusively to their work with patients have hitched their wagon to a falling star" (p. 3).

SEXUAL CONFLICTS AND THE
SEXUALIZING THERAPIST

Concomitant with the aforementioned shifts in our culture, particularly in the area of interpersonal relationships between men and women, have been rapid, perhaps revolutionary, changes in sexual behavior and attitudes (Hunt, 1974; Karasu & Socarides, 1979). People from all walks of life feel much freer than their forebears to bring their sexual conflicts and sexual unhappiness to the mental health practitioner (Strean, 1983) and to other helping professionals as well (Rutter, 1989).

Not only are more people willing to talk about their sexual lives and expose sexual conflicts and fantasies to a helping professional, but also a variety of sexual practices are now much more acceptable in the society. Premarital cohabitation and sexual intercourse, instead of being shunned, have been gaining increased acceptance by parents, college officials, even the courts. As was noted earlier in this chapter, "swinging," "switching," and group sex among the married are far from taboo in many sectors of American life. Homosexuality, formerly considered morally and legally reprehensible, is now legitimized as a "life-style" and is no longer considered a symptom of conflict by the American Psychiatric Association. Many therapists now advocate premarital and extramarital sex as avenues to mental health.

A superficial glance at just a few of society's major institutions leaves no doubt that our overt attitudes and sexual behavior have been drastically modified. In 1944 Professor John Honigmann, writing in the *Journal of Criminal Psychopathology*, stated that "sexual interaction in the presence of a third party would unquestionably be considered obscene in our society and indeed, our cultural norms would scarcely tolerate such a situation even in the scientific laboratory" (p. 721). Yet, two decades later, Dr. William Masters and Virginia Johnson were observing couples having intercourse in the laboratory and recording their physical and emotional responses (1966). In contemporary movies, the nude human body is constantly being exposed and sexual intercourse is frequently visible. Furthermore, accceptable language in the movies, theater, and literature has changed radically. Until the 1970s, sexual intercourse, the penis, and vagina, were only vaguely alluded to in the media. Now words like "fuck," "cock," and "cunt" are frequently utilized with limited objection from viewers and readers.

Describing the sweeping changes in our sexual mores that evolved during the 1970s, Morton Hunt writes: "Even in respectable literary works, descriptions of sex acts ceased to be indirect and poetically allusive, and became clinically graphic. Writers such as Philip Roth, John Updike, and Jean Genet included scenes of masturbation, fellatio, cunnilingus, buggery—oh, yes, and intercourse—of such explicitness that Lady Chatterley seemed second to Heidi" (1974, p. 7).

Along with the changes in sexual behavior and customs have been an increasingly wide variety of approaches to the understanding of human sexuality. As Karasu and Socarides (1979) note: "The resurgence of the neurobiological approach to sexual behavior and its reinforcement by data from bio-chemistry, pharmacology, genetics, and behavioral theories have tended to lead many away from the motivational approach of psychoanalysis into a more mechanistic behavior-oriented and social-engineering framework" (p. vii). Sexuality as viewed by many mental health professionals has become more of a bodily experience and less of an interpersonal experience governed by unconscious wishes, superego mandates, ideals, developmental experiences, and internalized objects, to name just a few concerns of the psychodynamic therapist.

A psychiatrist and psychoanalyst specializing in the treatment of women with sexual problems, Dr. Natalie Shainess (1979) points out that the sexual standards of today as they impinge on the mental health practitioner are set by business and commerce, which is why many people believe that pleasure can be mechanically induced. She further suggests that our media have helped us distort sex so that we erroneously conclude that sex can be separated from the individual's beliefs, personal myths, emotions, attitudes toward others, as well as the presence or absence of a degree of self-esteem.

Just as instant coffee is popular today, so is instant sex. According to many writers (Karasu & Socarides, 1979; Shainess, 1979; Strean, 1983), sex has not only become more mechanical, but also is increasingly a vehicle for the discharge of aggression rather than love. Expressions like "zipless fucks," "one-night stands," "getting laid" usually do not imply a fusing of tender and erotic feelings in a love relationship, but suggest a concern with narcissistic and bodily gratification with limited care given to the partner's needs.

One of the trends in today's society that has become a trend in the mental health field is to deny unconscious processes. Many clinicians have not been taking into sufficient consideration in their work with patients that the most conspicuous feature of human sexuality is that it is governed less by hormonal influence, statistics, changing sex roles, and other factors, no matter how important these factors might be, than by unconscious psychological events (Karasu & Socarides, 1979; Shainess, 1979).

If sexual behavior is primarily a motivated field, how can we understand what motivates our patients? In his *Three Essays on the Theory of Sexuality* (1905), Freud demonstrated that the sexuality of men, women, and children is strongly influenced by their developmental experiences. Whether or not an individual is able to enjoy a sustained and loving sexual relationship depends on how well he or she has resolved the psychosexual tasks appropriate to the various stages of childhood. Has the individual resolved the tasks of the oral stage so that he or she can trust the partner and be trusted? (Erikson, 1950). Is the man or woman able to kiss and gratify other oral wishes of his or her own and of the partner? Has the individual resolved the problems of weaning and separation-individuation so that autonomy of the self and of the partner are not too threatening? Have oedipal problems been resolved so that the individual does not feel too compelled to make the partner a parental figure? Can the person tolerate his or her own homosexual fantasies?

The fate of a person's sexual responses, whether the person be a patient or a therapist, is decided long before he or she engages in sex. The human psyche is formed early in childhood and the result is enshrined in the person, often without the individual's conscious knowledge. To understand what motivates people to behave sexually the way they do, we need to understand the vicissitudes of their psychosexual development.

It is the major thesis of this text that sexual problems of a man, woman, or child, whether the individual is a patient or a mental health professional, cannot be viewed as separate from the psychodynamics of the individual who has these problems. It is also a major contention of this text that the adult man or woman who has mastered developmental tasks such as trust versus mistrust, autonomy versus self-doubt, initiative versus guilt (Erikson, 1950) and who is comfortable with his or her oral, anal, phallic-oedipal, and homosexual impulses will be able to fuse tender and erotic impulses in a monogamous marriage. When the individual is not able to do this, like the practitioners in this study, he or she needs psychotherapy in order to resolve maturational tasks and unresolved neurotic conflicts.

Let us now meet these therapists and see how their own personal psychotherapy helped them mature sufficiently so that they could give up exploiting their patients sexually, begin to enjoy their own marriages, particularly the sexual dimension of their marriages, and start to like doing their work with patients as they worked more compassionately with them.

CHAPTER **II**

THE CASE OF
RONALD STERLING
A Macho Psychiatrist Afraid
of the "Woman" Within

It was late September. I opened the door of my consultation room to face a handsome man in his middle to late forties, impeccably dressed in a well-tailored blue suit, with matching shirt and tie. He was a little over six feet tall, slim, and walked erectly. He had a small mustache that, like the rest of his grooming, appeared to have received much care. Behind his friendly smile and warm handshake, one could sense depression in his face and tension in his movements.

Dr. Ronald Sterling, a psychiatrist in private practice, who had also studied psychoanalysis, walked from the waiting room with me to my consultation room, a place where I spend almost as much time as I do at my home. It is a comfortable room, quite spacious, and cheerful; it is located on 96th Street near Central Park West in Manhattan. When Ron Sterling entered the room, he looked at the analytic couch for a brief moment and as he walked toward the chair opposite the one where I usually sit asked, "I guess this is where I belong?" He followed this query with two more: "In this office, you are the boss, aren't you? Therefore, may I have this seat, sir?" I responded, "Help yourself."

As I silently reflected on Ron's opening remarks before we sat down, I wondered how comfortable he was feeling on becoming a patient. Did he worry about being asked to lie on the couch? Did I hear some muffled resentment in his voice when he referred to me as "boss" and "sir"? Did he really feel he "belonged" in the patient's chair inasmuch as he spent a great deal of his time being a "boss" in his own consultation room? And, what was going to be one of my consistent counter-transference problems in my work with Ron became apparent to me when I asked myself before anything was said by him, "Does he have any feelings about working with me, a non-medical therapist, inasmuch as he is a prominent psychiatrist?"

I stopped reflecting on my own preoccupations when Ron formally opened the interview by saying, "I'm familiar with your writing on marital conflicts and I have a very troubled marriage! I thought maybe you could help me to resolve my marital conflicts, or else help me decide to get a divorce." After a moment of silence, I asked Ron, "Could you tell me about some of your marital conflicts?" Overcoming what appeared to be an initial reluctance, Ron then spoke steadily for approximately 20 minutes about his very troubled marriage of 12 years duration.

"Although Adele and I had a blissful courtship and ecstatic honeymoon, things have not been going well ever since the honeymoon was over," Ron began. Then he continued, "I think we've become enemies because we are always arguing about everything. We argue about money; we argue about our seven-year-old son Robert; we argue about the fact that Adele works too many hours a week as a psychiatric nurse; we argue about our parents, in-laws, and friends. But, what we argue the most about is sex!"

Despite the fact that Ron and Adele enjoyed a mutually enjoyable sexual relationship during their two-year courtship, in their marriage they had abstained from sex for long periods of time, sometimes as long as two months. When they did get together, Ron frequently suffered from premature ejaculations. If Ron on occasion was able to sustain an erection, Adele felt he was not "tender" enough, and she would "turn off." Most of the time, Ron and Adele accused each other of being asexual and extremely insensitive to the other.

Although the Sterlings threatened each other with divorce constantly, they never separated during their 12 years of marriage. Arguments, though always verbal and never physical, were experienced by Ron as "real wars" followed by "armed truces." "Occasionally," reflected Ron, "it's worse than the United States fighting against Japan!"

Ron shared with me during his first interview that after one year of marriage he had almost daily fantasies of leaving his wife and going off with another woman. Occasionally, he would think of marrying one of his professional colleagues. From time to time he had fantasies of having an affair with one of his old girlfriends. Then Ron went on to say to me, "Because I know you are an open-minded guy, I have two things I want to tell you in confidence." He then asked, "I guess I don't have to tell you or ask you about confidentiality do I, Dr. Strean?" I realized that Ron was worried about how much he could trust me. Consequently, I asked him, "Are you a bit concerned that what you tell me won't remain just with me?" At first, Ron tried to reassure both of us by saying, "I know you'll keep everything to yourself." When I remained silent, Ron said, "I'm aware how much gossiping goes on in our field. Therapists like to talk to each other about their cases, particularly spicy cases that have to do with sex!" I told Ron that inasmuch as he just met me, he could not be sure just what I would do with his "spicy" material. (I was not aware that someday I would want to write a book on a subject on which this patient would provide material, and that he would be camouflaged so that even he would not recognize himself.)

With some mild pleasure and gratitude Ron exclaimed, "You don't bullshit or falsely reassure. I think I can trust you!" (I had learned rather early in my career that when prospective patients are not quickly reassured about their doubts in regard to therapy but are encouraged to talk about them, they often feel more understood by the therapist and can then talk about embarrassing issues with a little less anxiety.)

Ron then went on to tell me what the "two things" were that concerned him. "First," he said, "I have been unfaithful to Adele throughout most of our marriage. I've had a series of girl-friends—sometimes for just a few months, sometimes for a couple of years. I've had about a half dozen affairs with different women—most of them women I've known in my work. One or two were psychiatrists. The others were occupational therapists and social workers. I've never had an affair with a nurse. I suppose that says something, huh?"

Very much emphasized by Ron was the fact that sex with his partners outside of marriage "has been wonderful." Stated with intense enthusiasm, he said, "Other than with Adele, I feel potent and very much the man with every woman. I feel wanted, appreciated, and turned on—the opposite of what I feel at home. There are never any arguments with these women and I get a lot of reassurance from these relationships."

The other issue that Ron wanted to discuss with me were his fantasies toward some of his women patients. He found himself thinking about how fulfilling it would be to marry one or two of them and to have affairs with a few more. After discussing his sexual and marital fantasies toward his patients, Ron looked at me rather quizzically. His expression made me question whether he was concerned about my reaction to hearing his emotional involvements with his patients. Consequently, I wondered out loud about a seeming hesitancy in his delivery; then he became the erudite psychiatrist and said, "I guess I'm projecting my punitive superego onto you and wondering how much you are interested in admonishing and punishing me." I responded, saying, "I guess you are not quite sure whether I'm here to understand you or to judge you and maybe even to gossip about you."

Once more Ron seemed to feel reassured by my willingness to recognize and accept as real his doubts about me. He went on to tell me that he needed some help with some of his "countertransference problems with female patients."

The remainder of the first interview was spent by Ron telling me about his relationship with his son Robert. He said that Rob was "a good boy" but "there seems to be a lot of distance between us." Ron further reflected, "Every time I think of getting close to him, something holds me back. I don't know what it is."

Because Ron had some doubts about me and about going ahead with therapy, I did not want to pressure him to commit himself to fixed appointments or fees. Instead, I asked him if he would "like to talk a little bit further," to which he agreed with some moderate enthusiasm.

In our second interview, Ron spent a good part of the time discussing his relationship with his parents and with his sister who was two years his senior. He described his physician-father as a very authoritarian man who pressured him to achieve academically and athletically. Said Ron with tears coming down his face, "He didn't have much to do with me other than to prod me. He was a busy guy and did not have much time for anybody except for his patients." Ron went on, "He and my mother battled a lot. I don't think they loved each other very much. My mother used to confide in me and my sister that if it weren't for us, she would have left the old man."

Ron also mentioned in the second interview that his mother was "overprotective and too dependent on me for solace." During his teenage years and for some time later, his sister made him a confidante and often discussed with Ron her severe difficulties with men. When Ron began his work with me, his sister had already divorced two husbands.

Following Ron's remarks about his mother and sister, he returned to the subjects that brought him to me for help. He told me that he had mentioned to Adele that he was considering the possibility of returning for more therapy and that she was very encouraging of the idea. Ron added that he was surprised that they did not have an argument about his going into treatment because, as Ron had told me in the first interview and mentioned again, "We argue about everything."

It was during further discussion of his marriage, during his second interview, that Ron told me about some of his previous therapy. His last therapist was a woman who saw Ron and Adele conjointly in marriage counseling as well as in individual interviews. "It didn't work out," commented Ron, "because

Adele felt that the therapist was too much on my side. I think Adele had a point because the counselor kept telling Adele that she was very castrating and critical and that I wanted a more loving wife. Although it was true that I wanted and still want a more loving wife, she was too rough on Adele."

Ron also mentioned that he had a six-year analysis while he was in analytic training. His analyst, a male, was a senior faculty member at the classically Freudian institute that Ron attended. Describing his analysis, Ron pointed out, "I had a very positive transference toward him throughout most of the analysis. I got to some resentment toward my parents, particularly toward my father. My analyst liked me—I could tell—and I felt very supported. However, I know I did not resolve everything. I still have two 'marriages' most of the time and I'm too involved with my patients."

Inasmuch as I have found that I could learn a great deal about the major dynamics, conflicts, and personal strengths of a therapist when I could get a full picture of how he or she works with patients, I asked Ron for further details about his therapeutic activities. What he told me was very revealing. He was a very active clinician, frequently gave advice, and shared many personal revelations with his patients, including his sexual fantasies toward them. Although regarding himself as a Freudian psychoanalyst, his work deviated a great deal from the model of classical Freudian analysis. Rather, he seemed to be having very personal relationships with his patients that lacked the discipline and neutrality that most analysts feel is essential for the psychoanalytic process to work.

Near the end of his second interview, Ron proposed that we "get together a couple of times a week." He concluded, "I need your help." We agreed on the frequency of appointments and on a fee rather easily and amicably.

After the second interview, I wrote down some of my impressions and reactions to Ron. The following is verbatim from my notes:

"Dr. Ronald Sterling is a very troubled man. Though very bright and engaging, he has many doubts about himself as a man. He's involved in a very sado-masochistic relationship with his wife and experiences her as a rejecting mother. In the same profession as his authoritarian father, he has never resolved his resentment and competition toward him. Rather, I have the impression that he has submitted to father, has many homosexual fantasies toward him that he tries to ward off with a lot of promiscuous behavior. His mother, seductive but not too maternal, aided and abetted a strong, oedipal conflict that also seems unresolved.

"I think that his nurse-wife stirs up a lot of incestuous fantasies in him. That's why, I think, he can only enjoy sex away from the marital bedroom with his girlfriends who are not mothers. I believe that his excessive involvement with his patients reflects poor ego controls, severe sexual problems, and a great deal of unresolved hostility toward his former analyst.

"His inability to relax with his son suggests that he's frightened of the little boy in himself that yearns for a father. He wants a papa but is scared that there will be too much intimacy.

"I think his therapist liked him too much and, as a result, his hostility toward him and toward parental introjects has not been resolved. I'll have to watch this, too! I like him but I wonder why he wants to work with a nonmedical therapist. Should I have asked him? Was this some of my competition with him? I do feel sorry for his women patients (and men, too) who are not being helped but in many ways are being abused.

"He needs a lot of help from a father who does not indulge him or pressure him, but who helps him face his latent homosexuality, strong hostility, oedipal conflicts, much of which comes out in his marriage, his affairs, and his strong, destructive countertransference problems with his patients."

THE TREATMENT OF RON BEGINS

Initially Ron came for his twice weekly interviews on time and spent the first several weeks talking about his marital frustrations. He vascillated in his productions, moving from strong rage toward Adele to deep hurt and disappointment on facing how unloved he felt by her. He also went back and forth between wanting "to make a go" of his marriage or leaving Adele, getting a divorce, and finding another woman.

During the first few weeks of our work, Ron had a lot to say. Consequently, I listened attentively and said very little. This is what Reuben Fine (1982) has called being "dynamically inactive." Most individuals, particularly at the beginning of treatment, welcome a nonintrusive listener who gives them the opportunity to discharge pent-up feelings that have been held in for long periods of time. Usually when beginning patients can say what is on their minds without interruption, questioning, or comment, they feel accepted and their self-esteem begins to rise. This is what happened to Ron. After six weeks he remarked that he felt much less depressed and less tense. He was not arguing as much with Adele and he was finding himself feeling much more empathetic toward his patients.

In his seventh week of treatment, Ron asked if he could increase the frequency of his sessions to three. When I consented to this, soon after Ron proposed that he use the couch "because I really need intensive treatment."

Ron welcomed the "intensive treatment," associated freely, and began to talk a bit about how much he experienced himself in many of his close adult relationships as if he were a young boy. In the third month of therapy he had a dream that, upon analyzing it, disturbed him a great deal and shifted his transference to me from a predominantly positive one to one that was essentially negative. In the dream he was behind the couch, analyzing an attractive woman whose name was Harriet Stern. Harriet was describing her erotic fantasies toward Ron and both of them were sexually excited. On associating to the dream, Ron talked a great deal about his being "turned on" very frequently while he did therapy. He particularly found himself sexually excited when an attractive woman was lying on the couch. When I asked Ron who Harriet Stern was, he said he did not know anybody by that name, but "in the dream she looked like somebody I've met recently." To a question in which I wondered where Ron met Harriet Stern, he replied, "Although it seems farfetched, I feel I met her here in your office." With some help, Ron realized that, indeed, he had met Ms. Stern in my office. The initials of her name were the same as mine and the first and last names were also quite similar.

When I saw that Ron had accepted my interpretation that he had made me the woman analysand and made himself the therapist, I suggested that perhaps there was something uncomfortable for him lying down on the couch as a patient. Although he denied it at first, further reflection led Ron to the idea that "being on the couch makes me feel too vulnerable, too passive, too weak." He further suggested that as a therapist I could feel strong and potent but as a patient he could not. "As a matter of fact," exclaimed Ron, "being on this fucking couch makes me feel too feminine." I could then suggest to Ron that perhaps that was why he made me the attractive woman in the dream. Feeling like a woman on the couch was making him feel very uncomfortable.

Despite the fact that Ron consciously accepted all that we had unearthed from his dream, he began to attack me soon after "for forcing me to accept your interpretations as if I were a patsy." He further suggested that I must be a very passive fellow because I am a social worker and as Ron saw it, "Men who go into social work are effeminate and weak." Ron wondered further about my sexual identity and thought perhaps I was bisexual. As in his dream, he became my analyst and for many sessions offered several hypotheses about my psychodynamics. He told me I was a compulsive workaholic who wrote many books and articles in order to deny my strong wish to be very passive. Furthermore, he felt that I was very involved with topics like sex and marriage because I have problems with both. Finally, Ron was convinced that I made "aggressive interpretations," acted like "a rapist," at least with him, to ward off "much vulnerability" because I felt inferior to him. "I am a medical psychoanalyst, a graduate of a top-notch analytic institute and you are a lowly social worker from a half-assed institute," bellowed Ron in one session in the fourth month of treatment.

Although it would have been easy enough for me to ascribe all of Ron's "analysis" of me to "transference," to "projection of his bisexual difficulties onto me," or to some form of "projective identification," Ron had hit on some vulnerabilities of mine and made some accurate interpretations about me. It was important for me to delineate clearly reality from fantasy and transference from countertransference.

As Chused (1992) points out, many patients can take something very real about the therapist and use it in the service of the current transference. However, analysts and therapists can also take something very real about the patient and use it in the service of countertransference (Strean, 1993). Furthermore, under the guise of "doing therapy," all practitioners can act out countertransference feelings and fantasies of their own and consciously believe they are being helpful to their patients when they are really trying to protect themselves (Jacobs, 1986).

As I indicated earlier, I did feel somewhat "inferior" to the medical analyst that Ron was. During one of my sessions with Ron, I recalled a time when I was in a child analytic training program and remembered that I did essentially the same work and attended the same seminars as the psychiatrists did but I received one-third the amount of the stipend they earned. As I associated to my memory, I realized I was feeling about one-third as valuable as Ron!

Ron probably sensed some of my anxiety when he was blasting me and even may have picked up something in my attitude that reflected some of my competition with him. However, while reflecting on my countertransference issues and relating them to his transference productions, I became convinced that Ron was working hard psychologically to defeat and to humiliate me because he was worried that, like his father, I would humiliate and defeat him. My hunch tended to be validated in a session that we had late in the fifth month of treatment. In that session, Ron asked me, "Are you really that intimidated by me that you are frightened to argue with me?"

When I responded to Ron's query by saying, "I think I frustrate you by not arguing with you. I get the impression these days that you would rather I try to fight with you than try to understand you." Ron mocked my comments and derided my manner of speaking as if it were that of a naive woman. He repeated some of my words in a song-song voice, "I frustrate you. I want to understand you." He then went on, "Bullshit, Strean, you are a weak fairy!"

As the treatment moved into the sixth and seventh months, Ron continued to berate and to derogate me. Because I was becoming a bit better at mastering most of my counter-transference reactions, I could identify more compassionately with Ron's plight. I began to realize, and with much conviction, that what Ron was persistently doing to me must have been done to him by his authoritarian father, and with as much intensity and consistency. As I listened to Ron, he more and more reminded me of the angry child who had his tonsils taken out or a tooth forcibly extracted and went around playing doctor or dentist, doing the same thing in play to his peers that had been done to him. This wish of Ron's to hurt or castrate others the way he felt he was victimized is what Anna Freud (1946) aptly called "identification with the aggressor"—a defense used a great deal by traumatized children.

It was fascinating to me that as I was experiencing Ron more as an angry, hurt boy and less as an intimidating, authoritarian adult, in the eighth month of therapy he had several dreams about his son, Robert. In these dreams, Robert emerged as rather withdrawn, sad, weak, and vulnerable. Initially, Ron associated to these dreams by discussing with me how he had neglected his son and how he now realized how much the boy was crying out for help. He was also able to acknowledge that he had felt uncomfortable showing Robert physical and verbal affection because he had been "deprived" of these vital ingredients as a boy and did not know how to relate to a son. Eventually I was able to interpret to Ron that in his dreams, he was Robert, hungry for affection but feeling he could not show his yearnings to me.

Initially, Ron fought my interpretation, but he did not "protest too much." Soon he was able to talk about always wanting a father to support him, praise him, and hug him. With much courage and with much terror, toward the end of the first year of treatment, Ron could begin to talk about homosexual fantasies that he had toward me. In his dreams and fantasies, we took showers together, had oral and anal sex together, and became "asshole buddies."

As Ron used less energy fighting his homosexual fantasies and was more accepting of himself in general, he reported that his relationship with Adele had improved, he was getting along much better with his son Rob, and, aware of his identification with me, he reported, "I talk much less when I'm with my patients and I listen to them much more."

As in all treatment, the patient moves one step forward and then one backward (Fine, 1982). Sometimes the forward movement can induce so much anxiety in the patient that he or she can take two or three steps backward. This is what seemed to happen to Ron.

Although feeling somewhat liberated by facing some of his homosexual yearnings, Ron also became frightened by their intensity. Consequently, he felt he had to regress and act out. Following the summer break after a year of treatment had elapsed, Ron did seem pleased to be back in treatment and pleased to see me again. However, for many sessions he avoided talking about transference issues and instead became very involved in telling me about sexual conquests he made over the summer and into the fall. As Ron began to go into detail on how he seduced women colleagues, and how they fell passionately in love with him, I realized that he was deriving a great deal of exhibitionistic gratification in boasting of his "large and sustained erections," his "staying power" in intercourse, and "the shape" his "virile" body was in. I also became aware of the fact that by calling attention to his body in each session with me, Ron was secretly deriving some homoerotic pleasure. But, because his homosexual wishes were so threatening to him, he had to become a Don Juan (Fenichel, 1945).

Despite the fact that I knew that Ron was acting out his homosexual transference toward me with women colleagues, and although I felt tempted once or twice to confront him with that, I knew his dynamics well enough by now that, in all probability, he would take any intervention on my part as a command to cease and then would have to angrily defeat me. I learned from Ron in the first year of treatment that he was a very vulnerable, anxious man and felt very wary about anything I said, particularly if he did not have some conviction himself about the issue under discussion. Furthermore, Ron seemed so stimulated, anxious, and full of affect at the time that I felt the best way to help him was to listen to him carefully and wait until I felt he was in a psychological position to hear me.

The more I returned to my "dynamically inactive" stance (Fine, 1982) and carefully listened to Ron's associations, the more I realized that Ron was desperately trying to cope with an intense homosexual panic. After releasing many sexual fantasies toward me, his appetite for a loving, embracing father figure grew stronger but also unbearable. His promiscuity was a needed defense to protect him against much anxiety.

As Ron talked more about his sexual escapades, around the middle of the second year of treatment, with much hesitancy, embarrassment, and humiliation, he made what he termed "a difficult confession." He had been having an affair with one of his woman analysands for about six months. Although he felt very uncomfortable and guilty about it, he could now ask for my help in trying to understand his involvement with the patient. This ushered in a new phase in the treatment.

RON'S SEXUAL LIAISONS WITH PATIENTS

In contrast to Ron's bombastic and belligerent tone that accompanied many of his productions, when he shared with me that he was involved sexually with a woman patient, he appeared guilty, contrite, and somewhat depressed. He described his patient, Sylvia, as an attractive married woman about three years his junior who "made me feel like a perfect man." Sylvia obviously had a very idealized transferrence to Ron and experienced him as an omnipotent superman who was brilliant, sensitive, sexy, and very handsome.

Sylvia, who came into treatment with Ron because she had severe marital conflicts, sexual inhibitions, and difficulties on her job as a social worker, was convinced that if she could marry Ron, her troubles would be over. Ron told me that he tended to agree with her, and he also believed that most of his own difficulties would be resolved if he married Sylvia.

Despite Ron being very much in love with Sylvia, he was very conflicted about what to do with her. In the four times a week he was scheduled to see her, he would have regular therapy with Sylvia in two of the sessions, and in the other two he had sex with her in his office on the analytic couch. Inasmuch as Sylvia and Ron very much agreed that the sexual relationship was "therapeutic" for Sylvia, she paid for all the sessions. However, in the two past therapy sessions, Sylvia spent most of her time trying to convince Ron that they should have sex each time they got together. However, Ron felt that "this was a resistance to the therapy."

Ron tried to provoke me into punishing him for his "anti-therapeutic" activities. When he saw that I would not cooperate with him and punish him, but tried instead to understand with him why he wanted me to censure rather than to analyze him, he began to explore his motives for getting involved sexually with Sylvia. One of his dreams was quite revealing. In it, he had made Sylvia my patient and he was fighting with me over her. The dream ended in a boxing ring in which the referee declared Ron the winner and champion who had defeated me and won over Sylvia!

In associating to his dream, Ron recognized his strong oedipal competition with me, "the father figure." Not only did he want to take my woman away from me, but he wanted to defeat me in my work as a psychotherapist. Ron told me at this time, toward the end of the second year of treatment, that he really had a great deal of hostility toward "the psychotherapeutic establishment." He resented their rules and regulations and felt there was "nothing great about an analyst's abstinence." He tried to legitimate sex as a viable form of therapy. Argued Ron, "Who is to say that only talking is the answer?"

Ron was eventually able to recognize his fight with me and with the psychotherapeutic establishment as a derivative of a repressed fight with his father. He spent many sessions castigating his father for being so arbitrary, judgmental, and pressuring. Many memories were recalled from his childhood in which Ron was crying out for understanding and comfort from his father and received coldness and criticism, instead.

While recalling many sado-masochistic interactions between his father and himself as a boy and as a teenager, Ron could see more clearly how he was bringing this fight into his relationship with me and into his work as a psychotherapist. With this recognition, he began to see me more realistically and from time to time even felt that I was trying to help him, not hurt him. As we entered the third year of treatment, and while Ron was in a more positive transference, he told me one of the reasons that he sought me out as a therapist. He confided, "It was also my way of telling my medical colleagues to go to hell. I'll see Strean, 'a *lay* analyst' and they'll want to argue with me about it! I guess seeing you is part of my provocativeness, eh what?"

Whenever Ron's hostility diminished and he entered into a more positive transference with me, he always became frightened of his homosexual fantasies, particularly those toward me. By the third year of treatment, he was a little less intimidated by these fantasies and could talk about them more freely. In analyzing the dream that he had several months ago in which he beat me up in a boxing ring and took my woman, he was able to see that taking my woman away from me was also taking the part of himself that wanted to be a woman away from me. To face the woman in himself was Ron's strongest resistance and he was becoming more courageous in talking about wanting to be his mother and/or his sister with his father, rather than a threatening and threatened son to his father.

During the course of analyzing the part of Ron that wanted to be a woman with me, I could interpret Ron's affair with Sylvia as in part doing with her what he wanted me to do with him — have sex with him. Although Ron could accept this part of himself with a little more equanimity, his way of coping with it with his patient Sylvia was very interesting.

Ron said in the middle of his third year of treatment, "I realize that I'm acting out my transference toward you with Sylvia. It's not helping my treatment and it's not helping hers." In saying this, I thought Ron was going to give up his affair with Sylvia and either try to relate to her solely as a therapist or break up with her entirely and refer her to another practitioner. I was wrong. What Ron decided to do was to stop being Sylvia's therapist and to be her lover. Instead of meeting at Ron's office, they would get together either at a motel or aboard Ron's yacht. "This way," reasoned Ron, "my treatment won't be compromised. Further, Sylvia and I agree that her relationship with me is the best therapy she can have, so this seems to be the best arrangement for everybody."

Despite the fact that Ron had Sylvia and himself convinced that dropping her formal therapy and having an exclusive affair was not only an excellent compromise, but was "growth" for both of them, Ron was not sure he had me convinced. Although I did not say anything to encourage or discourage Ron's new arrangement with Sylvia, but tried my best to maintain a neutral stance so that he would be free to explore all of his options in a safe atmosphere, Ron projected his punitive superego onto me and had me very critical of him. "I know what you are saying to yourself, Strean," bellowed Ron in one session, "you are saying, 'That guy has not resolved a thing. He's just not treating her any more, but is acting out his transference even more.' But you are wrong, Strean, I'm trying to keep things cleaner and neater." On my maintaining my silence at this time, Ron then tried to get me to argue or to take some kind of stand with him. When I did neither, he became exasperated with me and said, "You are more interested in being an abstinent, neutral 'shrink' than a helpful colleague."

While Ron was advising me on what he was sure I thought of his new "arrangement" with Sylvia, I, of course, was trying to determine what he was trying to accomplish and was also examining my own feelings toward Ron and his current relationship with Sylvia. I felt that when Ron was having sex with Sylvia in his office and she was still his patient, it reminded him too much of his fantasies toward me. It appeared quite clear that when Ron was with Sylvia, the patient, in a therapy office having sex, it stirred up fantasies and wishes in Ron to be a "Sylvia" with me. Inasmuch as being a sexy woman with me was still too much of an unbearable idea to Ron, by making Sylvia a friend and not a patient, he would feel less threatened.

As I examined my feelings toward Ron at this time, I found myself empathizing with how desperate he felt about facing his conflicts. I felt sorry for Sylvia for being deprived of good therapy and had one or two fantasies of rescuing her and treating her myself. As I examined these fantasies more carefully, I realized that it was an expression of my own oedipal competition with Ron. I was going to show him how to treat a woman properly! He was the medical doctor who needed to learn from me!

By studying my countertransference reactions more carefully, I also got in touch with some of my feelings of anger and envy toward Ron. I was angry at Ron for devaluing his therapy with Sylvia and mistreating a fragile woman who needed a great deal of constructive therapeutic help, and for his attempts to deride me and to devalue our work. My envy of Ron, which took me a long time to face, had to do with his freedom to give immediate expression to his id impulses without examining them. Although I realized it was a manifestation of his desperation and anxiety, and despite the fact that I had known for a long time that instant gratification is a form of infantile behavior, I, nonetheless, secretly envied Ron's freedom to behave like an infant. Of course, what I really envied in Ron was a projection onto him of my own wish to be an infant. In reality, Ron was much too anxious and too guilty just to be a happy baby.

When Ron ascribed his critical and punitive superego to me and had me ready to censure him "for not treating Sylvia at all and having a full affair instead," I knew that interpreting his defense of projection would only make him more anxious and angrier. Consequently, I asked him why he thought I would be critical of his affair—what did I have against it? Ron told me that he was quite sure I valued monogamy and a talking therapy and would be against arrangements that were not honoring monogamous marriage and not respecting "the ethics" of psychotherapy. When I asked Ron for more details such as why he thought I adhered so loyally to monogamy and to an exclusive talking psychotherapy, Ron told me, "You believe that if someone has resolved his psychosexual tasks, he'll function the way you do. . . . I even read that stuff in one of your books so, Strean, this is not just a projection!"

It became clearer to me and a little clearer to Ron that he would not have to have me berate him so much or quote me so extensively on monogamous relationships and the ethics of psychotherapy unless he had real doubts about his new arrangement with Sylvia. However, I remained quite convinced that he had to discover these doubts by himself. Otherwise, he'd feel pressured and manipulated by me and would have to fight me.

As Ron continued to discuss what he thought were my objections to his affair with Sylvia, with the new arrangement about two months old and with his treatment nearing the end of its third year, Ron reported a new development in his relationship with Sylvia. With much embarrassment, Ron told me that he was quickly losing his sexual interest in Sylvia and he found that at least half the time when they had sex, he was impotent.

Ron became very depressed. Tearfully, he pointed out that he had been having the affair with Sylvia because it made him feel very masculine and more self-confident. "Being with her has been a boost to my self-image. Now, I dread it because I feel like such a weakling," lamented Ron.

As Ron and I attempted to analyze his sexual difficulties with Sylvia, we gained some new understanding about him. During our sessions, Ron found himself making slips quite frequently, calling Sylvia by his wife's name, Adele. He soon realized that his new arrangement with Sylvia made her appear more like a wife to him, and less of a girlfriend. As his psychological wife, Sylvia was less sexually interesting to him. On exploring this, I learned that both at the motel and on the yacht, Ron and Sylvia had meals together that Sylvia cooked. In addition, Sylvia perfomed some of the other traditional wifely chores such as cleaning and making the beds. Ron said, "This makes her less of a sexual person and more of a mother!" "Who wants to be a motherfucker?," asked Ron somewhat sarcastically.

It was while we were examining some of Ron's feelings toward his mother and starting to see how he had been making both Sylvia and Adele mother figures that Ron decided to break up entirely with Sylvia. Once again, Ron diagnosed his impulsive decision as "growth" on his part. He felt that it was about time he made Adele his one and only and made his patients "real patients." And once more, Ron had himself and Sylvia quite convinced that Sylvia should have some "real therapy." However, again he was worried that he had not fully convinced me that his "reasons for breaking up with Sylvia were mature." Stated Ron, "I don't think you have any serious objection to my breaking up with Sylvia, nor do I think you'll be too upset if I give up sex and confine my work with patients exclusively to psychotherapy, but you are not convinced that I'm doing this for the right reasons. You think I'm doing this because I have so many sexual difficulties with Sylvia that I'm ending the relationship with her because basically I am a narcissistic character disorder who can't stand being impotent." As was true throughout the therapeutic process, I did not either confirm or deny Ron's assessment of my position but tried to help him understand himself as well as possible and make his own decisions about his life.

THE EMERGENCE OF THE
MATERNAL TRANSFERENCE

When Ron stopped his sexual liaison with Sylvia, he did not have any sexual partners other than his wife, Adele. For about four or five weeks he felt quite comfortable. "I don't have to feel guilty about anything and I sort of feel I'm doing something right," confessed Ron. Although he was both sexually potent and tender with Adele, he was wary, nonetheless, about sustaining his current arrangement with her and wanted some encouragement from me that he could do so.

When Ron did not receive the approbation that he desired from me, he went into a depression that was deeper and more agitated than any of the others I had observed in him. In contrast to his derisive and contemptuous attitude that he frequently showed when he was frustrated by me, Ron was more tearful, felt more lonely, and acted very neglected. In a dream that he had at this time in which he wanted to borrow a book from my library and I refused, Ron experienced me as an ungiving mother. As he associated to the dream, very tearful as he did so, he talked about his mother who always seemed so involved with herself that she could show only little interest in him. Many times as a child he felt that he was just "a pest" as far as she was concerned. In contrast to his sister, Kay, Ron felt very unloved by his mother and told me that a song he often sang as a boy was, "Sometimes I Feel like a Motherless Child." Although his current relationship with Adele was now on "a more even keel," he was still worried about emerging as a motherless child.

In his relationship with me, Ron consistently experienced me as an ungiving, hostile person who was much more interested in my rules and regulations than I was in him. Session after session he would report dream after dream and fantasy after fantasy in which he felt extremely isolated, rejected, and unappreciated not only by me but by the whole world. In response to me and the world as an unfeeling, unloving, rejecting mother, Ron felt he had "every right in the world to feel hostile and vitriolic." Indeed, he was.

One of the positive side effects of Ron's reliving his relationship with his mother in the current transference with me was that the rage that he acted out in the past with his extramarital partners and with Sylvia was now being directed solely at me, his therapist. Now his relationships with Adele and with Rob were at their best. He was doing good work with his patients and he was enjoying his relationships with his colleagues and friends more than ever before.

Although I was pleased that Ron seemed to be mastering his conflicts much better and enjoying his life much more, his hostility toward me and toward his mother did not abate one iota. I noted to myself that when Ron made me his mother, I did not feel as conflicted as when I was experienced as the oedipal father. However, I felt troubled that the transference remained static.

It has been my experience, after many years of doing therapy, that when the transference remains static for a long period of time, whether the transference be consistently positive, negative, or ambivalent, something is going wrong! Either there is some undetected resistance of the patient's blocking therapeutic progress, or, some undetected counterresistance of the therapist's is doing the same thing. In the case of Ron, it was both.

During a session near the end of the fourth year of treatment, when I could not determine the reasons for our therapeutic impasse, I decided to ask Ron if he had any thoughts about it. While I was planning on asking Ron to help me understand what was going on, I was reminded of a case of a rebellious adolescent that I treated early in my professional career. This patient, despite his high intelligence, could not read, was extremely antisocial and friendless. He had defeated three therapists before he met me and it looked very likely that I would be the fourth. However, when I asked him what would help him in therapy, he gave me some sound counsel. One piece of advice that he offered has been of enormous help to me for close to four decades. Advised my young patient, "Don't talk so much, listen more!" (Strean, 1990).

When I asked Ron what he thought was going on between us that kept us in a perpetual struggle in which I seemed to be ungiving and unrelated to him, at first Ron experienced no difficulty in trying to help me. He informed me that he "had" to see me as an ungiving mother. However, soon after when he refused to try to help me figure out this impasse, I knew that his stubbornness had something to do with the rigidity of his current transference position. As Ron spoke more of his reluctance to help me, I began to understand that if he didn't continue to hate me, he would feel extremely vulnerable. Exclaimed Ron, "Why should I help you, you bastard and bitch? You never have given me very much of anything and now you want me to help you out while I give you an expensive fee! You give me next to nothing, and you want more for yourself! Screw you!"

Ron, as he felt with his mother, had to continue to hate me; otherwise, he would feel he had lost a crucial power-struggle. "I'd feel like a sweet little pussy cat submitting to a tiger if I stopped fighting you, " stated Ron vehemently. He continued, "I will not descend to the position of a needy child. That's what you would like me to do. I won't show you my neediness, even though it's in me. If I show you my neediness, I won't appear noble. I'm needy but I have to appear noble."

The resistance that Ron was expressing by maintaining his current transference position took the form of spiting his mother and me. Ron did not want to give either of us the opportunity to feel pleased with ourselves, even if that meant that he would not be helped in the therapy.

I had failed to see fully the enormous investment that Ron had in keeping me an ungiving mother. I realized that this was strengthened unwittingly by me because I had a strong investment in viewing myself as a giving mother. My counter-resistance, I began to realize, reinforced Ron's resistance. In effect, I was saying to Ron, "I'm a good mother. Accept my sweet milk!" He responded by saying, in effect, "Your milk is sour and

I won't drink it!" The more Ron sensed my desire to be a good mother, the more he rejected me, and the more I sensed his rejection of me, the harder I tried to help him.

On becoming more sensitized to my countertransference problems with Ron, I could be more appreciative of his current transference. I slowly realized that Ron was going through what Freud (1923) in *The Ego and the Id* referred to as the "negative therapeutic reaction." Here, Freud described the patient who freely associates, listens to interpretations, seems to understand them, but never makes much progress. Freud attributed the patient's lack of progress to his or her punitive superego that does not permit the patient the pleasure that would evolve if the neurosis was given up. As therapists have further studied the negative therapeutic reaction, they have learned that concomitant with the superego blocking pleasure is the patient's id wish clamoring to defeat the therapist (Fine, 1982). Usually, the more hatred the patient harbors toward one or both parents, the more the patient wishes to defeat the therapy and the therapist.

In my own study of the negative therapeutic reaction, I have often found that the therapist, usually quite unconsciously, is aiding and abetting the patient's negative therapeutic reaction through his own counterresistances, as became apparent in my work with Ron.

When I gained more mastery over my counterresistances, I could be more accepting of Ron's strong wish to keep me as the cold, narcissistic mother. As he discharged more hatred toward his mother and me and could feel more compassion coming from me, Ron began to try to understand his hatred better. Slowly, he began to realize that he used his hatred as a source of strength. Without it he felt castrated and very needy. In a dream during the early part of his fifth year of treatment, Ron made himself a young boy and made me his mother. As he moved toward me, he found himself becoming smaller and smaller. In another dream that involved Ron, and me as his mother, he became an adored girl, like his sister.

Ron's insight that to love a mother made him feel small,

vulnerable, weak, and like a little girl was very helpful to him in his relationship with Adele and with his women patients, as well. He began to see that when with a woman that he respected and with whom he wanted some intimacy, he turned the woman into his mother who would not enjoy his masculinity. As he found me to be a more accepting mother figure, he began to feel more comfortable as a man with women.

As Ron felt more relaxed and secure in his relationship with Adele and with me, he could initiate a productive examination of his past and present relationships with his female patients. He realized that by turning many of his female patients into mother-figures, he felt very weak with them. To overcome his sense of weakness, he felt compelled to be excessively seductive and overly sexual. In addition, Ron began to understand that quite unconsciously he often projected the little child in himself onto the women patients and he became their mother. As a mother, Ron experienced himself as if he were his own mother and then assumed his patients hated him. To cope with their imagined hatred, he either became too seductive or too aggressive with them.

TERMINATION

As we were completing Ron's fifth year of three times a week treatment, I felt he had made a lot of progress and that he was ready to terminate. I was quite sure that he himself was feeling somewhat ready to end our work, but I was also aware that neither of us had said very much about it. I wondered, "Why?"

On subjecting to self-examination what I felt might be a collusion between Ron and me in which we were mutually resisting facing the termination of treatment, I had hardly begun the process when Ron helped me see much better what was going on. His wife, Adele, had just begun her own treatment with a woman therapist, and he knew he was feeling anxious about it but found it difficult to analyze his anxiety with me.

As was often true of Ron, whenever he told me that something was difficult to face, he soon faced it. At first Ron thought that he would not be able to cope with Adele's changes that would emerge from her therapy, but after some further examination, that did not seem to be too much of an issue. Later, Ron wondered if, through her therapy, Adele would become rejecting of him. However, Ron told himself rather quickly that their marriage had improved a great deal and that Adele pointed out that she went into treatment because she wanted to learn how to love him more and enjoy sex more with him. He could really see that Adele was not the rejecting mother of his past.

When I suggested to Ron that he picture Adele and her therapist in his mind and see what his fantasies were, he accepted my suggestion and visualized Adele as a little girl with an adoring mother. He did not need my help to realize that the fantasy was an externalization of what a part of himself wanted to be—a little girl with an adoring mother, something that his sister Kay had enjoyed, at least as Ron experienced their relationship.

Recognizing that his fantasies about Adele and her therapist implied that he still wanted to be my daughter with me being his loving mother, Ron acknowledged that by trying to be my daughter, it was his way of resisting termination of treatment. Ron then spent many sessions talking about what "independence" meant to him. It had many negative connotations. It conjured up associations of being on his own, feeling pressured to produce academically and elsewhere, but never receiving the warmth and encouragement of his father, all of which made him feel very lonely and angry. Independence also brought associations to his mother who made him feel either too much like a rejected little boy or a pressured little boy who had to act "like too big a man." It also induced the obligation to be "a father-figure" for his sister, which he almost always resented.

In effect, Ron experienced termination of treatment as a rejection—a feeling that he shared with many other men, women, and children who face the end of treatment (Firestein,

1978). I was the father of his past who did not want him to be with me unless he produced for me. I was also the mother of his past who did not want him to be with me unless he soothed and comforted me. And, in some ways I was the sister of his past who did not want him to be with me unless he would be my confidante. Finally, I was the colleague and friend who wanted him to be replaced by another colleague or friend.

Because Ron had felt rejected by me, when he asked me if we could set a date for termination, I was very careful not to be too eager to comply. Rather, I asked Ron what he was feeling when he asked me to arrange a termination date with him. He replied, "We've got to get this over with! Why postpone the inevitable? I don't like the idea of ending our relationship and I probably never will like it."

Ron felt that his relationship with me had been serving several "worthwhile purposes." He pointed out that I had been his conscience and as long as he had to report to me, he knew he would not be in "too much trouble for too long." Here, he was referring to his sexualized countertransference problems with his patients and to his extramarital affairs that got him in trouble, largely with himself. Ron also pointed out that I had been serving as a benign superego for him—a warm mother and father—and he was reluctant to give that up. Finally, Ron mentioned how gratifying it was to "just say what's on my mind and see what I'm all about."

Although Ron had begun to face some of his resistances to terminating treatment, he still pressured me, although somewhat less, to arrange a termination date. When I suggested to Ron that inasmuch as he had a strong reluctance to end our work, why not try to understand his reluctance better, rather than try to suppress it. He welcomed my attitude and remarked, "When I know you are not so eager to get rid of me, I can face the issue a little more sanely." Now feeling more confident that I was not interested in rejecting him, he could more directly confront "the issue." What "the issue" seemed to be was his strong wish to feel like a lovable son of mine and his conviction that, without me, he'd feel like an orphan who could not cope with life on his own.

When we tried to better understand the feeling of being an "orphan" when he did not have me in his life, we learned that Ron would experience himself as an orphan because he had fantasies to kill me if I did not remain in contact with him and continue to be his loving "mother and father." He recalled the many times he felt like an orphan when he was a young boy, not realizing, of course, that his parentless status was a response to his death wishes toward his mother and father. Now, he was feeling similarly in his transference relationship with me.

As Ron continued to confront the little boy in himself that yearned for a symbiosis with a loving mother and father, more of his independent energies were released. What happened to Ron during the last phase of treatment had occurred throughout the therapy, namely, the more he faced his infantile wishes, particularly in the transference relationship with me, the more he could function as a mature adult in his daily life. I have found this to be true in my work with most patients. I think it is a good example of what Hartmann (1964) referred to as "regression in the service of the ego." When patients are able to regress in the therapeutic situation, feel and face the child within, they are enabled to feel more comfortable as adults outside of the consultation room.

Talking freely about his dependent, infantile feelings and his wish never to separate from me, and without me pressuring him to give up his symbiotic yearnings, helped Ron realize on his own, and with more conviction, that he could never be my little boy. As time went on, he began "to tire" of hearing himself talk about his infantile demands on me and seemed readier to end our work. He had been in treatment six years and by now we were both convinced his acting out with patients was "a thing of the past." We were also both confident that he would act and feel more consistently as a maturer therapist, husband, father, son, friend, and colleague.

ASSESSMENT OF RON'S THERAPY

In assessing Ron's therapy, I used as a barometer what I utilize in assessing all patients' treatment, both during the therapy and also during the termination phase, namely, Reuben Fine's (1982) "analytic ideal." It postulates that the mature, happy person should be able to love consistently in most of his or her relationships and harbor only limited hatred. He or she should be able to have consistent pleasure in life, but pleasure guided by reason, pleasure that does not hurt others. Sexual pleasure should be part of the mature and happy person's life, but again sexual pleasure that does not hurt others but is coupled with warm love. The analytic ideal further avers that the mature, happy person should be able to feel and express a wide range of emotions, is creative, can communicate well, participate actively and responsibly in a family and in the social order. Finally, the analytic ideal stresses that the mature, happy person is free of neurotic symptoms and/or other signs of emotional disorder.

Ron's sexual exploitation of patients was a sign that he was very far from the "analytic ideal." His treatment, which helped him move much nearer to the analytic ideal, had as its by-product the cessation of his acting out with patients. He found that, having had a sexual relationship with his patient Sylvia, he could not reestablish an appropriate therapeutic relationship and, in a difficult process, referred her to another practitioner for therapy. In order to cease his exploitation of patients, he needed a therapeutic and human relationship with a practitioner with whom he could identify, so that instead of abusing patients, he could treat them humanely. To do this he needed to become a humane, loving human being.

Dr. Ronald Sterling, after six years of treatment, emerged as a loving man with limited hatred. He could begin to enjoy himself much more with his wife and son, and his marriage became a monogamous one in which Adele and Ron enjoyed each other much more in all phases of living, including sex.

Ron, instead of using his patients to buttress his self-esteem, and acting out his hatred, began to enjoy his work: this was now doing effective psychotherapy exclusively. From a needy, narcissistic, childish person, he became a much more autonomous, loving, and mature man.

CHAPTER **III**

THE CASE OF ROSLYN MASON
A Psychoanalyst Who Administers Expensive Love Therapy

It was late in July, one day before I was to leave on my custom-ary five-week summer vacation, when I received a telephone call from Dr. Roslyn Mason. In a very businesslike manner, yet with some enthusiasm and warmth in her voice, Dr. Mason said, "Hello, I'm Dr. Roslyn Mason. You've been recommended to me by one of our mutual colleagues, Dr. Kay Samuels. Kay told me that you do one-shot supervisory conferences for analysts and therapists who have difficult patients. I have one of those. She's a tough one and I'd like to get on top of the situation. Usually I don't need much help to become comfor-table with patients and do competent work with them. So, I'd like to see you as soon as you can see me."

In rather sharp contrast to the way I usually feel when my supervisory or therapeutic assistance is being sought, as I listened to Dr. Mason's request, I could feel a fairly strong reluctance in myself as I thought about getting together with her. I asked myself if I was in such a hurry to start my vacation that just a little more work, even one supervisory session, would be too much for me. I was also a bit wary of a clinician who felt that just one meeting with me would enable her to work comfortably and competently with a difficult patient. Finally, inasmuch as I knew that most practitioners also took their vacations during August and were also winding down,

I wondered what was going on in Dr. Mason's personal and professional life. "Why is she looking for help now," I asked myself. I wondered why she wasn't doing what everybody else was, getting ready to go on her vacation.

My resistance to making an appointment with Dr. Mason became quite obvious to me when I heard myself answering her request, "I'm not sure I'll be able to help you in one session and I should tell you that tomorrow is my last day of work before a five-week vacation." I realized almost immediately that there was nothing receptive, engaging, or inviting about my response. I quickly noted to myself that what I said was a real turn-off.

But Dr. Mason persisted. She said, "Look, I'll arrange my schedule to come any time tomorrow. You just say what time you can see me and I'll be there." Feeling guilty about my initial response, and also identifying somewhat with her anxious plea, I found time in my schedule to see Dr. Mason the next day.

Although I was preoccupied with many matters, including saying good bye to my own patients and coping with our mutual separation problems, getting packed, and arranging for mail to be forwarded, I thought about Dr. Mason several times before I saw her for the consultation. She seemed more insistent than most people who seek me out. What was this about? As I reflected on how she seemed to be demanding and manipulative, I realized that I felt somewhat irritated with her. I also was very curious about what seemed to be a treatment crisis, and I even felt a bit challenged, though without my usual enthusiasm. "Quite a range of mixed feelings," I said to myself.

At the appointed time, Dr. Mason came into my office. She was about five feet five inches tall, wearing tailored and expensive-looking clothes, and she looked to be in her middle thirties (I later learned she was 39). It was quite obvious that she spent a lot of time on her appearance, with carefully polished long fingernails, very red lipstick, bleached-blonde hair, and ostentatious jewelry.

When we greeted each other, Dr. Mason shook my hand and said, "Hi, Herb. I'm glad we could get together. Your schedule is as crowded as mine so it's good that we worked things out."

She went on, "Kay Samuels who attended the same psycho-analytic institute I graduated from told me what a hotshot you were when it came to difficult cases. She said you helped her and some of our colleagues with the tough ones!"

Listening to Roslyn Mason's initial remarks, I immediately had some strong impressions. She seemed to be eager to have a "buddy-buddy" relationship with me and wanted me to know that she was a very experienced, well-trained, and busy prac-titioner. I recalled that over the phone she requested a "one-*shot*" session, now I was a "hot*shot*," and she seemed to want both of us to be "big *shots*." I wondered, "What is her anxiety about and will she tell me about it now that she's in my office?"

It did not take long to hear about some of Roslyn's anxiety as she presented her patient. "The woman I want to confer with you about is Joanna. She is 32 and came to see me about six months ago for marital problems. She finds herself turned off to her husband emotionally and sexually. For the first five months of treatment, the work was going swimmingly. But for the last four weeks or so, she's been very negativistic, has formed a negative transference, threatens to leave treatment, and is telling me that she is not being helped—which is a lie!"

As I tried to get a fuller picture of Roslyn's treatment of Joanna, I learned that Joanna was being seen twice a week and that Roslyn was "very successful in helping Joanna resolve many of her resistances toward aggression." Exploring this feature of the treatment, I learned from Roslyn that she had "verbalized many of Joanna's hostile feelings toward her husband for her." Roslyn had informed Joanna that she found it difficult to acknowledge to herself her husband's "severe limitations" and did not allow herself "to tell him off often enough."

Roslyn beamed with obvious pride when she informed me that her patient felt much "freer and more libidinal with the ag-gression that I loosened up for her." Referring to Joanna, Roslyn seemed ecstatic as she said, "She's had a couple of affairs for the first time in her marriage and is more orgastic than she's ever been. She has no children so a divorce would not be difficult."

When I tried to figure out with Roslyn what had happened to make her patient dramatically alter her feelings toward therapy or her therapist, Roslyn had no explanation. Since I could learn nothing about her patient's extreme shift in attitude, I asked a couple of questions which emanated more from a hunch than from substantiating data. I asked Roslyn, "Are you planning a vacation?" Matter of factly she answered, "Yes, next week I begin a four week vacation." "What has your patient had to say about it?" I queried. Roslyn was very quiet for about 15 seconds and then said with some embarrassment, "Almost nothing."

I next found myself sharing my puzzled reaction to Roslyn's saying that her patient had "almost nothing" to say about the vacation and blurted out, "There's something very strange about a patient being so attached to a therapist and then having nothing much to say about her vacation. I think she's defending against how upset she really is with you about your going away and that is coming out in her opposition to her therapy and you." Roslyn's response to my comments were as puzzling to me as was her patient's reaction to her therapist's vacation. Roslyn replied, "That's an interesting hypothesis you are making. You subscribe to Mahler's notion of separation-individuation and believe she is asserting her autonomy. Very interesting!"

I thought that Roslyn completely misunderstood me and that we were not communicating well. I was trying to tell her that her patient could not tolerate the pain of being away from her therapist and was coping with it by trying to demean her therapist and the therapy. Roslyn, I thought, could not face the patient's pain in separating from her and, like the patient, had "almost nothing" to say about it except for some extraneous theoretical speculations. I wondered, "Was Roslyn having some difficulty separating from the patient? Does separation from her patients stir up issues that she has not fully resolved? How come she's so damn intellectualized?"

For many years I have observed in my colleagues and myself that whenever we are very preoccupied with a particular patient, that patient probably has activated a current conflict in us. Frequently I have noted as well that just as descriptions of a son or daughter by a parent are usually autobiographical references to the parent, albeit unconscious ones, statements about a patient by a therapist in supervision are frequently references to the therapist's own unique dynamics. For example, when a mother or father says to a therapist, "My child is not responding to limits," we invariably learn that the parent is having difficulty in setting limits at the particular stage of the child's development. And when a parent tells a practitioner, "My son (daughter) needs some new sexual information these days," the practitioner usually learns that the parent these days needs some sexual information too (Feldman, 1958; Love & Mayer, 1970; Sternbach, 1947; Strean, 1978; Strean, 1979).

Supervision of therapists and psychotherapy of parents have a great deal in common. When a therapist brings a patient to the supervisor, he or she, like the parent, is usually expressing a disguised cry for help and is tacitly saying, "This patient (who is like a son or daughter) poses problems for me. The problems the patient poses are difficult for me to help the patient resolve because they are similar to my own unresolved issues." Consequently the supervisor of therapists, like the clinician who works with parents, must try to get in touch with the unconscious wishes, defenses, and superego injunctions of the therapist and try to determine the nature of the anxiety in the therapist that is blocking the flow of the therapeutic process. Just as parents who get help with their own problems with aggression can better limit a son or daughter, so, too, therapists who have received help with their anxieties can better help patients with the same problem. Furthermore, if the supervisor does not help the supervisee resolve his or her idiosyncratic conflict, the supervisee will not help the patient. Like the blocked parent who cannot help his or her child mature, the blocked therapist cannot help his or her patient move forward emotionally (Sigman, 1985; Strean, 1991b; Teitelbaum, 1990).

By the middle of my consultation with Dr. Roslyn Mason, I was silently asking myself several questions: "If Roslyn cannot help the patient cope with the pain of separation, what is it about separation that bothers Roslyn? What can I do to help Roslyn feel more secure about revealing her separation anxiety to me, so that she can help her patient do the same? How far away is Roslyn from knowing that she has overidentified with her patient, Joanna, and has formed too powerful an alliance with her in damning Joanna's husband? Does she realize that she's encouraging the patient to fight with her husband, rather than helping her to analyze her marital conflict? Is she aware of the fact that she is aiding and abetting the patient to act out sexually? What does this say about her own sexual conflicts? Is there a latent homosexual transference-countertransference struggle here?"

With so many questions deluging me, I also had to figure out what should take priority in the 20 minutes or so before Roslyn's consultation would be over. A moment before I concluded that I had to work with Roslyn right away about her own separation anxiety if I was going to help her at all, I had a useful insight. Just as I was feeling pressured to do something quickly for Roslyn, she was feeling pressured to do something quickly for her patient. And just as I was in the dark about how Roslyn was feeling about separation from her patient, Roslyn was equally vague about her patient's separation anxiety. With so much unsaid about vacation separation, I wanted to get Roslyn to talk about *feelings* of separation. She seemed so action-oriented (Sigman, 1985; Strean, 1991b).

Relating to what seemed to be the crucial issue, I said to Roslyn, "I've never found it easy to know when and how to tell patients I'm going away on vacation. Sometimes I can feel myself coming close to stammering!" Then I asked, "How do you go about it? And, do you remember specifically what you said to Joanna about your vacation?"

Roslyn turned red and became silent. After 30 seconds, I commented, "I think I made you uncomfortable." Roslyn said, "Yes, you did, but it's not fully your problem; it's also my former analyst's!" She pointed out that her analyst, a male, "did not handle separation issues in the usual Freudian way, even though he is a training analyst at the most ultra-orthodox psychoanalytic institute in New York." With a little more prodding on my part, Roslyn told me how her analyst handled informing his patients about his vacation plans and how she had "emulated his style and procedures." Referring to her analyst, Roslyn said, "Every year around June 30th, Sydney put a sign in his waiting room, giving the dates of his vacation. If I did not talk about his vacation, that was my privilege. But I always knew when he'd take off for the summer. And, I do the same thing with my patients. Actually, what is happening with Joanna often happened to me. She's seen my sign about my vacation and has not talked about it. And I usually did the same."

To myself I yelled, "Wow! This Sydney was afraid to talk about his vacations with his patients and now he's reinforced Roslyn's phobia of the same issue. What he didn't face in himself, he couldn't help Roslyn face. And now she's doing the same thing with Joanna. It's like a grandmother who is afraid of the dark imposing it on her daughter, who then imposes it on the grandchild. Holy smoke!"

Although I found myself feeling angry at Sydney for his irresponsibility in inflicting his problem on his patients, which was being recapitulated ad nauseum, I knew I had to be careful and to monitor my feelings. Otherwise, I would not be able to help Roslyn with Joanna and probably with her other patients, whose separation problems were being ignored, as well. I said to Roslyn, "There are probably few therapists who do not recapitulate with their own patients what they experienced with their own analysts or therapists. I bet you even post a sign similar to Sydney's." Roslyn laughed at this and said, "I bet you handle vacations different from the way I do! You probably verbalize the issue, don't you?" I told Roslyn that she was correct and wondered out loud what she thought of the way I went about it. She told me, "Quite frankly, I'm ambivalent. I can see how it could help someone like Joanna who may miss me." I agreed with Roslyn and said, "Since you've been working on her aggression, you may want to consider bringing the aggression into the transference relationship and suggest that maybe your unavailability for four weeks has stirred up some angry feelings toward you."

In what I now saw was Roslyn's quite detached and intellectualized way of coping, she responded to my suggestion by saying, "Perhaps if she can verbalize some part of the latent negative transference, she'll get to her negative introjects and deal with the separation anxiety from what Melanie Klein calls 'the bad breast.' I further agreed with Roslyn and told her that I thought whatever she could do to verbalize the patient's hurt, anger, and probable feelings of rejection, it would help to preserve the treatment. I suggested further, "Just as she now wants to reject you, I think she might be feeling rejected."

At the end of the consultation, Roslyn thanked me for "the time," wrote me a check, and said that she would think over our "chat" and see how or if she would use some of it in her work with Joanna. In departing she said, "Maybe we'll bump into each other at a conference." I answered, "Maybe."

After Roslyn bade me farewell, I assumed I would never see her again in my consultation room, though maybe at a conference. Though it was scheduled as a single consultation, Roslyn made enough of an impression that I gave some thought to her afterwards. Roslyn had seemed to be trying very hard to be autonomous and not eager to be dependent on me or anybody else. I felt that she was quite loath "to take me in" and I wondered how receptive she was to any man, maybe to any person. I had not observed such intense anger toward a patient's spouse as I saw in Roslyn; perhaps more disturbing to me was the fact that she did not view her contempt of her patient's husband as a countertransference problem.

I realized that I had gotten to know very little about Roslyn; I knew next to nothing about her personal life and little about her professional life. I did not learn, for example, whether or not she was married and what the term "next to nothing" was all about, which she and Joanna and I had all used. Did Joanna feel like "next to nothing"? Did Roslyn feel the same way? Did I feel "next to nothing" during the consultation with Roslyn?

These questions remained unanswered, yet I was reasonably certain that there were elements of truth in all my conjectures. I felt very critical of Sydney, Roslyn's analyst, because of the way he handled his vacations with patients and wondered what else was not confronted properly in Roslyn's analysis. Surely, I thought, Roslyn and Sydney did not face termination issues and this may have been a factor in forcing Roslyn to be pseudo-independent in her interaction with me, Joanna, and others. I also hypothesized that the unresolved termination issues in Roslyn's analysis may have reasserted themselves in her work with Joanna. Roslyn seemed insensitive to how Joanna was feeling about her vacation and did little to help her with it.

Critical of my own work with Roslyn, I realized, in hindsight, that I gave her too much advice to absorb. Of more importance, since she was very reluctant to take me in, I should have been more sensitive to her resistances. Perhaps, in part, because I had only one session with Roslyn, I was in too much of a hurry to sensitize her to too many things, and that is never helpful to anyone.

A REQUEST FOR MORE SUPERVISION

It was a surprise for me to hear from Roslyn in September, a few weeks after I returned from vacation. Over the phone in her detached, businesslike matter, she said, "This is Dr. Roslyn Mason. You will recall our meeting in July when I spoke to you about my patient, Joanna. I used a couple of points that we came to in our conference and it did pay off. I'd like to see you again about another difficult case."

When I heard Roslyn's voice, I had a very different reaction from the one I did when she first called me. In July, I felt irritated and pressured. This time I found myself feeling compassion and a wish to help. I remember saying to myself that although, in all probability, she was experiencing a lot of anxiety in her work with patients and probably in her life as well, she found it difficult to acknowlege this to herself or to others. I also recalled Roslyn's work with her analyst Sydney and felt quite convinced that she had many unresolved issues but did not feel courageous enough to return for more personal therapy. Supervision, I conjectured, was her only way of getting help right now.

Roslyn and I agreed on a time for another consultation. The case she wished to discuss this time involved a married man in his early forties who was having sexual problems. The patient, Al, had been impotent with his wife during most of their 10-year marriage. Although he had a girlfriend with whom he had an enjoyable sexual relationship, Al felt very guilty about his extramarital affair and was very ambivalent about continuing it. Despite the fact that he seemed to have related well to Roslyn during the year he had been in weekly treatment, when he resumed therapy after Roslyn's vacation, Al wanted to quit treatment, believing that his work with Roslyn had not been of any help to him.

As I listened to Roslyn's presentation, I realized that her second case had much in common with the first. Both patients had marital and sexual problems. Both formed very positive relationships with Roslyn but rather abruptly became very negative toward the treatment and the therapist. The first patient became furious before the summer separation and threatened to quit treatment; the second patient did the same immediately after the summer vacation.

It has become virtually axiomatic in the theory and practice of psychotherapy that when a practitioner is having difficulty with two or more patients with similar problems, unresolved conflicts of the practitioner are playing a significant role (Lane, 1990; Sigman, 1985). This axiom became reaffirmed for me as Roslyn told me more about her work with Al. As she had done with Joanna, she "verbalized for Al his latent resentment toward his wife." And, as she had proudly told me about her work with Joanna, she was pleased that Al could now enjoy extramarital sex much more. Finally, just as Roslyn had nothing much to say about how Joanna and she had coped with the summer vacation, the same kind of unrelatedness seemed to take place with Al.

As I silently reflected about Roslyn during my second conference with her, I realized that if she were to help her patients with the issues they were presenting, she needed help with her counterresistances (Strean, 1993). I reasoned, however, that she would be very wary of looking at herself in front of me and that she would not easily take responsibility for herself. "How can I make it safe for her to face her counterresistances with me?" I asked myself. I knew I had to be very tactful and tentative; otherwise, Roslyn would feel threatened, if not trounced. The more I listened to her, the more I knew she felt like a vulnerable girl and that her intellectual demeanor, detachment, and seeming independence were defenses that were not working too well for her. I also thought that she was having sexual problems of her own, and I wondered about her own marital conflicts or whether or not she was married.

In the middle of our second consultation, keeping in mind Roslyn's strong need to feel like a colleague who was definitely my equal, I asked her, "When you conceptualize the therapeutic process in your teaching and elsewhere, do you place much emphasis on counterresistance?" In what I now knew was her characteristic manner, Roslyn cited many references from the literature on countertransference and counterresistance. She also informed me of a class she had taught on "Counter-transference Issues in Marital Conflicts." I now knew what to say. "As a teacher, if a therapist in your countertransference class on marital conflicts brought you the cases of Al and Joanna, what would you do?" "Clever question, Herb," Roslyn replied with a mildly sarcastic smile, "But I'll help you out. I'd probably wonder what marital and sexual problems the cases provoked in the therapist. If the therapist wanted to review some of these problems with me, I'd listen, and then link up the therapist's issues with what was going on in his or her work with patients."

After a silence of about 10 seconds, Roslyn queried, "Should we do that?" I responded, "To quote Dr. Roslyn Mason, a teacher of countertransference, 'If the therapist wants to review some of these problems with me, I'll listen.'" Roslyn laughed heartily in response and I laughed with her; the laughter was spontaneous for both of us and I think at that moment we felt a little closer to each other.

Roslyn went on to tell me about some severe marital conflicts she had been experiencing throughout her 12 years of marriage. For the last five years, Roslyn and her husband Peter had no sexual relationship whatsoever. Though they were college sweethearts and enjoyed each other throughout their courtship, during most of which Peter was a psychiatric resident, soon after they got married, "things went bad and now we have little going for us at all." Both Roslyn and Peter were very attached to their eight-year-old daughter, Molly, who had "kept the marriage from breaking up."

With the time allotted to us for this second consultation having elapsed, I told Roslyn we had to stop (in what seemed to me the middle of her story) and asked if she would like to come in again and talk some more. Without any visible reluctance, Roslyn made another appointment for a few days later.

Roslyn then spent three sessions with me discussing more about her marriage. She described Peter as a successful psychiatrist who was very competent in his work as a hospital administrator and researcher. She also mentioned that he had "little use for psychoanalysis and psychotherapy." What bothered Roslyn the most about Peter was that he was very "threatened by [her] success and achievements and demeaned [her] accomplishments." They disagreed about many "important issues" — politics, psychotherapy, child rearing, and the role of women in society and in the family. "He's very conservative and I'm a solid liberal. Our respective philosophical perspectives stimulate much tension between us," stated Roslyn with rancor.

Inasmuch as Roslyn had been in analysis with Sydney for several years (it turned out to be four times a week for six years), I wondered to myself what had she learned about herself as a wife. In her sessions with me she appeared similar to the spouse who has not been in therapy and tends to project all of the interpersonal conflicts onto the marital partner. Roslyn seemed to be "a collector of injustices" (Bergler, 1960) who felt victimized but who was convinced she had not contributed anything to her demeaned status.

After reflecting to myself on Roslyn's past personal therapy, feeling that she was ready to talk about it, still carefully choosing my words, I asked, "Did you spend much time in your work with Sydney looking at your marriage?" Roslyn responded, "That's a good question and the answer is, no. Rather early in the analysis we discovered that I had married my sadistic mother and Sydney helped me see that I did not have to submit to my 'mother's' vengeance." I noted to myself here that in the same way that Roslyn was tacitly encouraged by her therapist to oppose her husband, she did the same with the patients she had discussed with me.

Roslyn informed me that she and Peter had agreed several years ago to have "an open marriage." By that Roslyn meant that she and her husband had mutually agreed that they would both feel free to have sexual partners outside of the marriage. "Although I've only had a few short term affairs," Roslyn pointed out, "they have been worthwhile." When I asked her if she could comment on some of the differences between Peter and her lovers, Roslyn mentioned that what she valued most about her extramarital affairs was "the rich and warm communication with these guys which was so different from what has gone on with Peter." She had little desire to discuss with me her sexual activities with her paramours, and I did not pursue the matter, trying my best to respect her resistances.

During our sixth consultation, Roslyn started the session by asking, "How would you feel if we changed our relationship?" I was not sure what she had in mind; to be a patient, a friend, or what. I realized rather quickly that in our recent sessions she felt more like a patient of mine than a supervisee, but I still experienced her strong wish to be a buddy and colleague. "What do you have in mind?" I asked. Roslyn said that she had found our "conversations" helpful and she would like to see me on a weekly basis; she would like to discuss "transference, countertransference, and resistance issues that emerge with my patients, and I'd like to take a look with you at some of my life issues as well."

Although I was not totally surprised when Roslyn made her request for treatment (mixed with supervision), I did not feel fully comfortable with the idea of seeing her as a patient. There were two major reasons for my hesitancy. First, there was something elusive about her. She started off wanting "a one-shot" consultation, moved toward having a few supervisory sessions, modified the supervision, and went on to discuss her many marital conflicts. I wondered to myself, "Where are we headed now?" Inasmuch as she seemed to have trouble committing herself to a marriage, and because she described two relationships with patients that went from intense positive relationships to possible abrupt terminations, I wondered what whould happen between Roslyn and me. Therapeutic work with Roslyn, I was quite convinced, was not going to be a smooth journey—it was probably going to be quite turbulent. I did not know if I was capable of being the kind of therapist she needed, one who could weather many storms and not lose his cool.

There was something else that was making me even more dubious about seeing Roslyn in therapy. I had learned over the years that moving from supervision or the classroom to therapy can be problematic. Supervision and other forms of teaching-learning relationships are usually much more gratifying to the parties involved and the interaction is usually much more spontaneous than occurs in sound, disciplined therapy. Also, in the classroom and supervision, the teacher is more self-revealing than the therapist is in the treatment situation. Therefore, when a supervisee or student moves into the role of patient, the transition is almost always frustrating, particularly for the patient, but also for the therapist. I was worried that Roslyn could not withstand the frustration inherent in the transition. With my activity that had taken place in the supervisory hours, I would not be the traditional "blank screen" that is prescribed for the therapist and I felt that Roslyn had already received some questionable therapy.

As I reflected some more about seeing Roslyn in psycho-therapy, I recalled the many treatment disasters described in the professional literature when the therapist abdicated his blank screen neutral role. I thought of Freud's treatment of his own daughter (Gay, 1988) and wondered what would have happened to Anna Freud if she were treated by someone other than Sigmund Freud. Perhaps her love life would have been more fulfilling. I also thought about some of the founding fathers of psychotherapy, who as patients had therapists who were undisciplined with them, and how they in turn acted out with their own patients. This was certainly true of Jung, Rank, Ferenczi, and Jones (Grosskurth, 1991). Would I be aiding and abetting Dr. Roslyn Mason to become another bright, acting-out therapist?

While thinking some more about whether it would be helpful if I were to see Roslyn as a patient, I recalled Roslyn's persistence when I was quite reluctant to see her before my summer vacation. She would not easily take "no" for an answer then, and I was quite sure it would not be any different now. Con-sequently, I knew I had to be sure and secure about my stance with her. This was not going to be easy because I realized I felt a bit intimidated and pressured by her. I had also noted in myself a couple of times some competition toward her when she seemed like a "know-it-all."

The more I obsessed about my ambivalence, the more it seemed like a good idea to try to enlist Roslyn's help in resolving some of my doubts. Therefore, I said to her, "Up until now we've been concentrating primarily on your work as a therapist, and I've seen myself as your supervisor. How do you feel about modifying our roles?" Roslyn responded, "I think we com-municate well and whether we talk about patients, transference, countertransference or the weather, we are still communicating." I felt Roslyn's comment revealed some real motivation for treatment, but I was still feeling my doubts. "As you know, talking about patients or the weather will be different if we become patient and therapist. I'll be talking a lot less, and you a lot more. And, we'll be spending almost all of our time trying to understand the whys and wherefores of your productions." Roslyn responded, "Look, if I don't like what you do or say, you'll hear from me about it. If you're too quiet, and by the way, I've heard from some of your patients that you are quite capable of that, I promise I'll level with you."

Although I found Roslyn's responses to my queries helpful in moving me toward a positive decision about being her therapist, I still felt somewhat manipulated. An association I had at the time which I did not analyze was going to prove very pertinent in my work with Roslyn. I do remember vividly that when I was on the verge of telling Roslyn that I would work with her in therapy, I said to myself, "I feel as if I'm being pressured into having an affair with her and I'm really not sure it will be good for either of us." So without fully feeling that I was the best therapist for Roslyn, particularly since we had a supervisor-supervisee relationship over a few months, I told her I would be glad to give therapy a try and we would evaluate from time to time how helpful it was for her.

THE TREATMENT BEGINS

At first Roslyn and I met once a week. Prior to the inception of our formal therapeutic work, I asked Roslyn for some of her history. I learned that she had "a sadistic mother who was cold, aloof, and very competitive with me. She resented nurturing me but seemed to adore my younger brother, Marvin." Although Roslyn's mother was described by Roslyn as uninvolved in her life, she was very critical of Roslyn's clothes, speech, friends, "and anything else that she could point to that would make me feel upset with myself." Roslyn described her father as a man who was very frightened of his wife. Though he was capable of more warmth than his wife, Roslyn was quick to point out, "He was so busy trying to please his wife that he did not have too much time for his children." Marvin, two years Roslyn's junior, now married with three children, "was resented because he was obviously preferred." Marvin and their father were dentists who shared an office.

Roslyn told me that she had always excelled in her studies. "Beginning in kindergarten and through my doctoral work and analytic training, I've always been on top." In contrast to her outstanding achievements as a student and practitioner, Roslyn said she was "a loner" who had very few friends throughout her life.

After I had listened to Roslyn's history and realized how emotionally impoverished her life had been, I felt a great deal of sympathy for her. My irritation with her pedantic and detached attitude, as well as my competition with her as she tried to impress me, seemed to vanish as I recognized how hurt and unloved she had felt most of her life.

For the first three months of Roslyn's treatment, she used most of her time telling me how disappointed and discouraged she felt as she thought about the important relationships in her life. She felt a great deal of distance from her family. This was the story of her marriage and even with her daughter Molly she felt "a lack of spontaneity and closeness between us." She could not really "trust anybody."

As is true with most individuals when they begin treatment, Roslyn had a lot to say and I felt the best thing I could do for her is what is usually best for most patients—listen empathetically and say little. Roslyn told me that she welcomed what she termed "my earnest interest"; but she also saw herself as my supervisor and colleague in certain ways, because she followed up her expression of gratitude by saying, "I know you've been very much influenced by Reuben Fine. I think he was your mentor. And you use his notion of 'dynamic inactivity' with expertise. Congratulations!"

During the third month of therapy, Roslyn brought in her first dream. In it she was approaching an older woman who seemed quite maternal but was guarding her breasts, and Roslyn could not see them, even though she wanted to see and touch them. Roslyn associated to the dream, talking about her "ungiving" mother who had something to offer but made herself inaccessible. Roslyn discharged much hostility toward her mother's "bad breast." She pointed out with some sarcasm that the psychoanalyst Melanie Klein, who coined the term "bad breast," was thinking about Roslyn's mother when she wrote about the phenomenon.

Inasmuch as Roslyn had already talked about her mother's unavailability and the dream's setting sounded quite similar to our current therapy situation, I felt reasonably assured that behind the dream's manifest content she was telling me that she was experiencing me in the transference as the inaccessible mother. When Roslyn talked about several teachers and "other mentors" as having more to give her than she was given, I knew it was appropriate to ask her if perhaps she wanted more from me than she felt I was ready to give.

After a few evasive remarks, Roslyn told me that she guessed she did want something from me but she wasn't sure I would want to give it to her. Since Roslyn had already shown that being given to was a very conflicted area of her life, I wanted to be thorough but move very slowly. Initially I worked with her resistance to talking about being gratified by me (Fenichel, 1945) and pointed out that I realized that what she wanted from me was quite difficult to discuss. Roslyn acknowledged that revealing to anybody what she wanted made her feel like a vulnerable child with her ungiving mother. "It's humiliating, demeaning, weakening, and frightening to ask for anything," stated Roslyn vehemently.

It took several sessions until Roslyn felt free enough to ask, taking a deep breath, sitting up erectly in her chair looking like a fierce warrior, "I want to come here more often!" After a long silence I asked Roslyn what she was feeling. She thoughtfully said, "It's as if you won a battle! I've shown you that I need you and now I know you are feeling stronger than I do. I am not as fiesty and formidable right now as I like to appear." After I listened to Roslyn's proclamation of defeat and followed her further associations, I was able to help her see that she was experiencing me as a big, strong mother and saw herself as a weak, small child who was now overpowered by me. Roslyn agreed and was able to see how she had felt weakened whenever she was dependent on someone but did not fully realize that she was recapitulating her relationship with her mother almost every day in many different ways.

Roslyn moved from once a week therapy to twice a week. By the end of six months of work she was seeing me three times a week and began to use the couch. Her transference prior to using the couch was essentially a positive one in which I was experienced mostly as the mother she always wanted — listening, attentive, and noncritical. Toward the end of her sixth month of therapy she said in one sentence what represented a complex set of feelings, "Everybody needs tender love and care from a mother. You are the first 'mother' I've ever had."

ON THE COUCH AND THE
NEGATIVE TRANSFERENCE

Although Roslyn eagerly went to the couch, after about four or five sessions of lying down she moved from a position of loving and appreciating me to despising and depreciating me. Obviously, the analytic situation where she could not see me was experienced by her as very different from sitting up, seeing, and conversing with me.

Being on the couch meant to Roslyn that she was the abandoned baby who had been deserted by her mother. In one of her dreams she was shouting and crying continuously in my waiting room, while I was not coming out of my office to be with her but made her wait indefinitely. Roslyn told me that, like her mother, I made myself invisible and unavailable and did not give a damn about her suffering.

In another dream, Roslyn was reading one of the books I authored and as she read the book she vomited. In associating to her dream, she told me that what I had to say, whether it was in her sessions or in my writing was like her mother's sour milk. It was distasteful and when she took it in she had to spit it out.

I knew it was very important for Roslyn's emotional growth that I be as accepting of her hatred toward me as I could and that I try my best to give her nothing in reality that would cause her to think that I was like her critical mother. When Roslyn observed that I was not retaliating when she was very hostile, she tried to provoke me into behaving as belligerently toward her as she was to me (Schafer, 1983). She found my neutral attitude frustrating and wanted to frustrate me. Consequently, she came late for her sessions, bounced checks, was defiantly silent in sessions, and was very critical of everything about me from my speech, dress, therapeutic interventions, office decor, the books in my library, and the towels in my bathroom.

When I told Roslyn that she seemed to be working overtime trying to draw me into a battle, she responded to my interpretation by telling me I was a coward, afraid to be combative. As she became more critical of me for being "weak," "too soft," "schmucky," and "vulnerable," I realized that she was resenting me more for being too phallic—too much like her image of her phallic mother, father, and brother. In one of her dreams, around the ninth month of treatment, Roslyn used a bow and arrow, shot at me, and made me bloody in the genital area. In another dream around this time, Roslyn and I were in a relay race. She stole the baton from me, kicked me, tripped me, and then got on top of me and beat me up.

From her associations, I was able to interpret to Roslyn that she wanted to castrate me, use my penis for herself, and then rape me while experiencing me as a woman. "Do you expect me to agree with you, asshole?" asked Roslyn belligerently after considering my interpretation. When I did not answer her question and remained silent, Roslyn persisted in her attacks. She told me how incompetent I was as a therapist and that she had already arranged two consultations with other practitioners to discuss leaving me and trying another therapist.

I knew that Roslyn's manner of acting out her negative transference by seeing consultants to help her decide about leaving me was a continuation of her attempt to provoke me into a battle. I also knew she felt very ambivalent toward me; otherwise, Roslyn would have just terminated treatment with me. When I suggested to her that she must have been feeling very torn about staying with me, Roslyn acknowledged her ambivalence. She told me that she had not forgotten about my nonpunitive, accepting attitude, and she also knew that I wanted to help her. "But," said Roslyn, "I do not think you are competent enough to help me. I need somebody who is more creative and who can take more initiative in the treatment. You are much too passive!"

Roslyn's demeaning me, berating me, and derogating me continued well past the first year of treatment. Despite my knowing that she was trying to put me into the castrated, weak state of mind that she felt within herself, her constant attacks were not always easy for me to take. However, I knew I had to monitor my own resentments and understand whatever castration anxiety I experienced in her presence. I became increasingly aware of how difficult it was for Roslyn to allow herself to be a full sexual woman with me, and it was also equally difficult for her to permit me to be a sexual man in her presence.

Roslyn's resistance to feeling like a sexual woman with me came through in one of her fantasies that she reported in her eighteenth month of treatment. Prior to a session while sitting in the waiting room, Roslyn fantasied herself on the couch with me lying next to her, but she refused to respond to my warm embraces. Here, I interpreted to Roslyn that although she had wishes to have sexual contact with me, she also wanted me to stop in the middle. I asked what made her want me to stop in the middle. Roslyn told me that she felt that she would be too passionate for me, too excited, and that I would feel too overwhelmed by her. Consequently, by stopping love-making in the middle of it, she was protecting me!

THE EROTIC TRANSFERENCE

As I helped Roslyn confront her resistance to facing her sexual fantasies about me, she became more open with them and seemingly more comfortable in telling me how much we could enjoy and enhance each other. Listening carefully to Roslyn's fantasies of "making mad passionate love for hours" and concomitantly "sending each other out of this world to Mars," I was struck by two features of her associations. Although she appeared more interested in seeing me as a sexual man, I felt there was a strong aggressive quality to her seductiveness and a lack of tenderness and sensuality. As I watched her manner of relating to me, I was reminded several times of Karl Menninger's (Menninger & Holzman, 1973) statement that an inherent part of a very erotic transference is a wish to demean the therapist and remove him from his professional helping role.

The other quality that seemed apparent in Roslyn's way of relating to me was that it lacked the "as if" quality that usually accompanies the therapeutic interaction. Almost all patients and therapists recognize that transference fantasies are wishes to be understood, not proposals to be gratified. However, when Roslyn talked to me about what she wanted to do with me sexually, she seemed to lack an observing ego and was not trying to understand herself. Rather, she appeared to be like an aggressive woman "on the make."

As I was considering how to help Roslyn understand better what she was really feeling and experiencing with me, she seemed to confirm my hypotheses. In her twentieth month of treatment, she made a real sexual proposal. She thought it would help both of us to have "a brief affair." She would then feel like more of an equal to me and this would help her resolve a life-long problem that always made her feel inferior to men. "An affair would help us," Roslyn added, "in that you would feel more loved and appreciated as a man."

When Roslyn told me that she was not interested in a long-term affair with me, but rather something like "a one-night stand," I was reminded of how she approached me for supervision. She wanted a "one-shot" deal. The same phallic aggressiveness that seemed apparent in Roslyn almost two years earlier was even more apparent now. She seemed more interested in "scoring and winning" than in making love.

The more Roslyn realized that I was more interested in understanding her wishes, defenses, and anxieties than in gratifying her, she made more and different kinds of requests, such as having a meal, writing an article, or teaching a class together. She pointed to many therapist-patient dyads that she knew about that had extratherapeutic contacts and insisted that "nothing horrible happened to them." Roslyn even thought it helped them.

I told Roslyn that it was not clear to me why at this time she was so interested in moving away from our therapeutic relationship and instead wanted us to be colleagues, lovers, friends, or something other than patient and therapist. Roslyn responded in a manner that puzzled me. She said, "With all of your training and experience, you still do not realize that a therapeutic relationship consists of two human beings who should learn to love each other in breadth and depth. When you go on interpreting, instead of being a human being who is a friend, you are abdicating your responsibility as a humane therapist and decent person."

The reason that Roslyn's statement puzzled me is that although she was a therapist with many years of training, experience, and personal analysis, she was advocating with enormous conviction a very unprofessional and untherapeutic approach. It seemed inconsistent with everything else she appeared to stand for.

As I was trying to understand Roslyn's strong desire for extratherapeutic contacts as well as her conviction about the legitimacy of them, realizing that her strong persistence and demandingness was an expression of anxieties, fantasies, and resistances that we had not worked on, she had a dream that helped clarify what seemed puzzling to me. In the dream, Roslyn was in her own office in a therapy session with a male patient, Doug, who was refusing to talk. Doug was a man who reminded Roslyn of herself in some respects because he was "feisty and formidable," "needed some reassurance" so that he could feel he was "lovable and sexual." Roslyn pointed out that the dream recapitulated a recent session with Doug in which he would not talk about something that he thought would meet with Roslyn's disapproval.

Realizing that when therapists dream about their patients, their patients are usually stand-ins for themselves (Fine, 1982), I suggested to Roslyn that perhaps there was something on her mind that was difficult for her to tell me. Roslyn then told me that she had been holding onto a secret ever since she began her work with me. It was very difficult to share the secret with me because she was quite sure she would receive my strong disapproval.

THE SECRET

I told Roslyn that feeling it was quite dangerous to tell me a secret that would bring my strong dispproval must have put her under a constant strain with me. Roslyn replied, "A truer interpretation was never made," and went on to tell me that a day had not passed in which she had not tried to force herself to tell me the secret but could not do so. "It was too humiliating," Roslyn said.

As I listened to Roslyn talk about the anguish, anxiety, and fear of reprisal that she had been trying to cope with for two years and thought about the pain she had been enduring, I felt a great deal of sympathy for her. However, as she continued to talk about how difficult it was for her to contain her secret and how much she anticipated my censure, I began to feel teased because she seemed far away from actually revealing her secret.

Fortunately, I had some experience in dealing with patients' secrets. Not only had I learned rather early in my training that all patients have some secrets they withhold from their therapists for some time (Fine, 1982), but also I had treated a man who came to see me several times a week for over a year and refused to tell me his name—it was a secret (Strean, 1991b).

I learned that part of keeping secrets from the therapist is usually a wish to tease, control, and exasperate the therapist (Greenson, 1967). Although the patient's fear of retribution is genuine, I became convinced that the fear of retribution was secondary to the patient's wish to torment the therapist.

Consequently, when I had enough data to say so, I told Roslyn that she seemed to want to torment me with her secret. I was quite uncertain about how Roslyn would react when she heard my interpretation and I was somewhat surprised to hear her say, "Yes, I do want to torment you. I've been tormented the last couple of years, and before that too, and I want you to know what it feels like!"

I believe that when Roslyn reminded herself that in all probability I was not going to pressure her to reveal her secret nor was I going to punish her for what she would disclose, she began to mobilize herself to tell me what she had been withholding. Initially, Roslyn informed me that she was planning to tell me the secret when she first sought me out for supervision, but she could not feel safe enough at that time. She believed I was "too ethical" and she wasn't sure what I would do—maybe "report" her for her "transgressions."

It was when she moved from being a supervisee to a patient that Roslyn thought she might be able to tell me her secret. "I felt as a patient it would be easier, but it had not been safe enough," Roslyn reflected. Then, in a session on about the second anniversary of treatment with me, Roslyn confessed her secret with what appeared to be only moderate anxiety. "I've been doing with my patient, Doug, for three years what I've wanted to do with you. I've been having a love affair with him." Doug, Roslyn told me, was an unhappily married man who came to see her because he wanted help with his troubled marriage. As Roslyn worked with Doug and saw how lonely, depressed, and needy he was, she "empathized deeply with his plight." On her own initiative, she hugged him after a session in which he had cried about missing a loving mother and yearned for a loving wife. "The hugs continued to be more regular and frequent," said Roslyn with much warmth and tenderness in her voice. She continued, "I felt that Doug, just a few years younger than I, would benefit from a loving woman who admired him for his intelligence, supported him in his business initiatives, and appreciated him sexually."

In Roslyn's initial rendition of her affair with Doug, she

seemed to be making herself sound extremely altruistic. It was as if Doug needed a warm, loving, sexual woman and Roslyn gave him what he needed, much like a physician supplies an ailing patient with the correct dosage of the appropriate medicine. Yet, I wondered to myself, "What was in it for Roslyn?"

As Roslyn continued to elaborate on her affair with Doug, it became clear that she derived a great deal of narcissistic satisfaction from the relationship. At times she sounded quite grandiose when she made statements like the following: "I have felt that Doug's depression lifted because of me. He can cope with a sadistic wife with much more ease because of me. His self-esteem has risen because of me. He's a new man because of me."

The relationship between Doug and Roslyn seemed to evolve into an extramarital affair in which the two people are secretly enjoying themselves away from their spouses and the rest of the world. They saw each other three or four times a week at Roslyn's office and had "a double session," conversing face to face for the first 45 minutes and having sex for the next 45. They talked a great deal to each other about each other, constantly reminding one another that each was a perfect sexual partner and an outstanding human being.

Doug, a successful businessman with an excellent income, paid Roslyn a high fee for all the "therapy sessions." It did not bother Roslyn too much to collect a high fee from Doug because she always felt the relationship that she provided Doug was "extremely remedial and very therapeutic." What did upset Roslyn was the fact that the fee she received from Doug was higher than the fee she paid me. She felt that she was "showing [me] up" and "winning whatever competition I've had going with you." Roslyn also felt uncomfortable paying me a lower fee than Doug paid her because she was quite convinced that I worked much harder with her than she did with Doug.

Roslyn's associations to our respective fee arrangements not only revealed her strong rivalry with me but also demonstrated her strong attempt to justify her liaison with Doug by implying it was a "love treatment." By constantly doing so, she could avoid examining her own motives that propelled her emotional and sexual involvement with her patient. In addition she could sustain the relationship without experiencing overwhelming guilt. Yet, the fact that she could not tell me about the liaison for two years, always anticipating my censure, did suggest that a great deal of guilt was present in her, though she worked hard not to face it.

What motivated Roslyn, at least in part, to discuss the affair with Doug in her treatment with me was that Doug was pressuring her to divorce her husband and marry him. This put Roslyn into tremendous conflict and she spent many therapy hours weighing the issue. In doing so, Roslyn gained some understanding of what precipitated her affair with Doug.

Despite being sure that she had "never felt so much in love and never felt so loved," Roslyn realized that her three-year relationship with Doug was very different from what would occur in marriage. Roslyn mentioned that when she and Doug were with each other, they were at their best. Roslyn could feel like a loving, nurturing, and eminently desirable woman while "running the show," and Doug could feel nurtured and taken care of and be able to "give up the controls." What turned out to be one of the major motives involved in Roslyn's affair with Doug was that she could feel "stronger than the man and still feel like a desirable woman." The competition and power struggle that were an inherent part of her marriage with Peter were obviated in her affair with Doug.

As Roslyn seriously reflected on the possibility of marrying Doug, she also noted that in her current arrangement with him she could "have the joys of marriage without many of the responsibilities." By this Roslyn meant that she could be loved, have enjoyable sex, but not have to deal with the mundane activities and everyday living problems that were an inevitable part of marriage. Furthermore, Roslyn pointed out that in her current liaison she enjoyed the many hours of independence and distance she had away from Doug, and that would certainly not be the case if she lived with him. Several times Roslyn wondered if she would experience him in a living relationship as an overbearing mother who would become sadistic like her own mother was with her. She also believed she would compete with him as she did with her brother, her father, and with me. "You know," Roslyn suggested, "how marriage revives the past. Maybe it won't be any better with Doug than it was with Peter."

Roslyn also realized that getting married to Doug would rob her of "the secret defiance" that took place in her affair with him. She told me that throughout her affair with Doug she felt a certain amount of "smugness" toward me, "secretly rebelling against convention." Prior to her treatment with me, she also enjoyed a certain triumphant feeling over her previous therapist, Sydney, as she "opposed the establishment."

Another strong motive in Roslyn's "love treatment" of Doug was that she gave her patient what she wanted to receive from me and her previous therapist. Reflected Roslyn, "What we can't receive, we give, and then vicariously identify with the receiver." By the time Roslyn was well into her third year of treatment, she said, "In going through all of the stuff of wanting to have an affair with you and now realizing its impracticality, I'm not sure how much it helps anybody."

While Roslyn was considering the pro's and con's of marrying Doug, she also reflected on what she had derived from her treatment with me. She felt that in working on her "hatred, competition, dependency problems, and bisexuality, I get along much better with Peter." At times she was aware of the fact that she and Peter were "quite warm" with each other, which helped her daughter Molly feel much more "relaxed."

During much of Roslyn's third year of treatment while she was examining her relationship with Doug and trying to understand better her mixed feelings about marrying him, Peter received an offer of a prestigious appointment in which he would administer a department of psychiatry at a medical school "far away from New York." At first, the offer to Peter seemed to be an answer to Roslyn's dilemmas. However, when Doug realized that Roslyn was seriously considering moving out of town with Peter, he protested strongly. He even threatened to sue Roslyn for her "unprofessional conduct." Doug pointed out that when Peter would hear about her affair with him, he would divorce her, she would lose her license to practice psychotherapy, and Roslyn would then have no other alternative but to live with Doug. Roslyn responded to Doug's threats by telling him that he probably was harboring a great deal of hatred toward her if he was so ready to sue her and wreck her life. Hearing this, Doug took Roslyn's statement seriously and withdrew his threats. Instead, he thought he would take up residence in the city where Roslyn was intending to move. He was not sure whether he would divorce his wife, but he was quite adamant about moving "with Roslyn" to continue their relationship.

Although Roslyn began to see many benefits in moving out of town with Peter and Molly, such as "starting all over again with Peter" and believing they could now "enjoy each other more or less consistently," she was willing to consider with Doug the possibility of his moving to the city where she would live. She "weighed the pro's and con's with him as you did with me." Despite the fact that Roslyn was quite insistent that she was doing this for "therapeutic" reasons, I thought that Roslyn would not give up Doug as easily as she made it sound. When her associations turned my hypothesis into something quite apparent, I shared this observation with Roslyn. Somewhat to my surprise, Roslyn said, "I still cover up my wishes by assigning therapeutic motives to them."

When Doug saw that Roslyn was planning to stay with Peter, he began to try to separate from Roslyn. This was taking place while Roslyn was separating from me.

TERMINATION

Although I would have preferred to work with Roslyn longer than we did, I tried my best to help her have a fruitful termination process even though it was limited to three months.

Roslyn was able to bring out some sad feelings about ending our work but spent most of her time enthusiastically expressing her gratitude toward me. She tended to cope with her separation from Doug in the same way, voicing some sadness, shedding a few tears, but recognizing that her "mutually gratifying" love affair was "too much of a departure from reality."

When Roslyn's defense against her affect was apparent during termination, I pointed this out as the same tendency during treatment. Roslyn noted that this defense was her way of coping with her "yearning to be mothered and fathered which was rarely forthcoming." I told Roslyn that because she would not have me or Doug in her life, she was trying to be "a superwoman." This interpretation did help Roslyn mourn me, Doug, and her parents somewhat, and enabled her to be less critical of herself for missing those she loved.

Roslyn felt that what helped her the most in her work with me was getting in touch with her sexual conflicts. She felt that by learning to accept herself more as a woman, she did not "have to prove it anymore." Although she found it difficult to cope with what she termed my "frustrating attitude," it helped her in her work with patients and her marriage.

ASSESSMENT OF ROSLYN'S THERAPY

Using Fine's (1982) "analytic ideal" to assess Roslyn Mason's progress in therapy, I felt that although she was much more genuinely loving, there was still some unresolved hatred in her toward parental introjects. Her sexual life and her role in her family and in society improved a great deal. As we noted in the termination phase, Roslyn was not able to communicate with a wide range of emotions. She tended to inhibit many of her affects and left treatment with some remaining arrogance and a tendency to intellectualize. I was not fully confident that she could sustain her therapeutic gains nor was I sure her marriage would continue to be mutually satisfactory.

One opinion, in an article "Physicians, Heal Thyselves," by Barbra Streisand (1992), producer and director of the film, *The Prince of Tides*, defends the character Dr. Susan Lowenstein, whom she portrayed in the movie. Dr. Lowenstein did have a sexual liaison with her patient's brother, Tom Wingo, and in describing Dr. Lowenstein's personality, Streisand writes:

> She is also a woman with her own problems. I chose to play the character of Lowenstein because she is a wounded healer. I know she exists, this woman capable of healing others yet needing help herself. Imperfect, human, like the rest of us. Where is it written that doctors have to be perfect, have to be gods? (p. 14)

In another point of view that pertains to Roslyn's liaison with Doug as essentially motivated by what Gabbard (1991) has referred to as "the love cure fantasy," Gabbard suggests:

> A recurrent theme in female professionals who have become involved in unethical sexual conduct is a powerful and pervasive fantasy that love is curative. . . .The scenario frequently begins as a rescue attempt and is then transformed into a misguided love affair. . . . [The female therapist] unconsciously believes that she can give the patient the nurturance that she failed to receive from her mother. . . .
> Psychoanalytic or psychotherapeutic investigation of therapists in this situation often reveals an overidentification with the patient. Many of these therapists feel they, too, were victimized by abusive or neglectful parents when they were children. The therapist's overzealous rescue of the patient and subsequent lovesickness may symbolically represent an effort to give the patient the love that the therapist did not receive as a child. Thus, the patient's and the therapist's need become tragically confused. . . .
> A female clinician is often drawn to [her male patients with whom she has sexual liaisons] with an unconscious fantasy that her love and attention will somehow influence this "essentially decent" young man. (pp. 1–3)

What Roslyn Mason learned is that a "love cure" is indeed a fantasy that needs to be understood rather than acted out.

CHAPTER IV

THE CASE OF
BOB WILLIAMS

A Psychologist-Sex Addict Who Believes His Women Patients Hunger for Him

I was leisurely reading *The New York Times* at my home on a Sunday morning when I was interrupted by a telephone call. "You don't know me by name. We travel in different circles," said the voice at the other end of the line. I wondered to myself, "Who is this mysterious caller beginning a phone conversation in a rather unusual way? Perhaps this is some kind of crank call."

Responding somewhat aggressively, I asked, "May I know with whom I'm speaking?" "Yes," said the voice, "as I told you, you don't know my name because I'm affiliated with a different psychotherapeutic group from yours, but I'd like to get together with you."

Even though the caller implied that he was a professional colleague, I noted that the gentleman still had not identified himself. "Why does he want to get together with me? Why is he calling me at home? Doesn't he realize that I do all my work at the office and not at my home on a Sunday morning?" My silent, impatient questions were ones I would like to have bellowed at the caller.

As I was posing these questions to myself, the caller finally became more revealing. "I'm Bob Williams, a psychologist, and I'm on the faculty of the Riverfield Psychotherapeutic Training Center.* I'd like to meet with you and discuss some pressing

*a pseudonymous title

professional issues." Although the seemingly mysterious man had now identified himself, I still did not know if he wanted to have a chat with me about some mutual training concerns regarding students, or whether he was considering me for a role in some conference, or just what. What was on Bob Williams's mind was still quite vague to me even after we had conversed for several minutes.

I then decided that I was going to be more direct, so I asked, "Dr. Williams, could you tell me the nature of the professional issues you would like to discuss?" He replied, "Sure. You can call me Bob. To answer your question, though, I'd like to discuss some sexual issues with you."

With each exchange, I was becoming more baffled. I was also becoming increasingly irritated. It was a Sunday morning, a time to get some precious and needed relaxation, and instead I had to contend with some stranger who seemed to be playing games with me. I felt anger at what I felt was a "tough character" but plodded on with resignation.

I then asked Bob Williams, "Are you interested in having an exchange with me on some of our mutual professional concerns or exactly what?" In response, Bob laughed loudly and heartily and said, "Well, you could put it that way, but what I had in mind was to discuss parts of my own sex life with you. Are you game for something like that?"

It slowly began to dawn on me that because I received Bob Williams's phone call at my home, I resisted facing the possibility that he was calling as a prospective patient who was having difficulty asking for a consultation. When this reality finally hit me, I asked, "Are you calling me for a consultation to discuss some personal issues?" "You got it!" Bob exclaimed enthusiastically, as I understood his point at last. I then commented, "Perhaps you don't know that you've reached me at my home?" "Oh, sure, I know I've reached you at home. I wouldn't expect you to be at your office on a Sunday morning." With a tone of surprise in my voice, I queried, "Is there some reason why you wanted to arrange for an appointment by calling me at home?" "Oh, sure," said Bob again, but this time more matter of factly, "I knew I could reach you directly at your home on Sunday morning, but during the week I would get your answering machine." "A clever manipulator is this Bob Williams," I remarked to myself. But I also reminded myself that it would not be helpful to him or to me to acquiesce to his request and do some professional work at my home on a Sunday morning, even if it were only to go over my working schedule with him.

Feeling quite convinced that I would be starting off on the wrong foot with Bob Williams if I made an appointment with him from home, I said, "I'll be glad to make an appointment to see you at my office if you could call me there during the coming week." It was clear that Bob was not going to accept boundaries or limits easily and he stated, "Look, Herb, I want to see you soon. Let's take care of making the appointment right now. It'll be off both of our minds." Using his formal title as a way of letting him know he was too informal with me, I rather firmly responded, "Dr. Williams, I do not have my appointment book here with me. I realize I'm frustrating and disappointing you, but I can probably work out an appointment for this week if you can call me at my office early in the week."

Bob was not going to be easily dissuaded. "Don't you know your patient schedule in your head?" he asked. Before I could reply, he went on, "Schedules are usually the same from week to week. I know exactly when my free time from patients is. Don't you know yours?" I thought to myself that even I if knew my schedule by heart, right now it would not be a good idea to make an appointment with him. "It's no emergency," I said to myself sharply, and repeated to Bob, "If you can wait until tomorrow and call me at my office, I'll do my best to find a mutually convenient time so that we can meet for a consultation."

When Bob seemed convinced that I was not going to be talked into making an appointment from my home, he reluctantly but somewhat ingratiatingly said, "Okay, Herb, I'll get you tomorrow!"

I went back to my *New York Times* but could not concentrate on the paper. Instead, I kept thinking about Bob Williams, who had not only intruded into my home on a Sunday morning, but now was intruding into my thoughts at a time when I did not want to think about work.

One of the ways that I try to solve conflicts and help others to do the same is to face as honestly as possible what is creating the anxiety and tension when it is occurring. As I began to associate freely to my phone conversation with Bob Williams, I not only realized that I was very angry at somebody who disrupted my private life, but also I was leery and frightened of my caller. He was quite evasive about why he called and his evasiveness induced some paranoia in me. My paranoia was exacerbated when I thought about his repetitive references to "sexual issues"—something most people do not even allude to once over the telephone.

As I reflected more about Bob Williams, I slowly realized there was something about my reaction to him that I was embarrassed to acknowledge to myself. I envied his "chutzpah" (nerve). My style in relating to others, which goes back to my early childhood, has been one that emphasizes a deep concern and respect for the other person's needs and wishes. Consequently, knowing that one of the last things in the world I would do is call a professional at his or her home on a Sunday morning and demand an appointment, I became aware of the fact that what I usually inhibited in myself, Bob was acting out; and I secretly admired his unabashed freedom, however intrusive, disruptive, and impolite he was!

I also could acknowledge eventually that I was irritated by Bob's informality. He was calling me by my first name before he even met me. "More intrusion!" I noted to myself. However, I also admired and envied his freedom to act like an equal of mine without any of the usual restraints that I show toward those whose help I want. This was another feature of Bob's modus vivendi that filled me with a certain awe as I thought further about him.

About 15 minutes after I ended the phone conversation, I told myself that there was something about Bob Williams's manner that made me wonder if he would call back as he had agreed to do. His demanding and manipulative way of relating induced in me the thought, "He seems to want what he wants when he wants it and if he does not get it, he probably fumes and runs. He's probably an "impulse disorder." Maybe I think he won't call back because I really don't want him to?"

No sooner had I concluded my conversation with myself when I began to feel guilty. I thought I was too abrupt with Bob, more irritated than I should have been, and I realized when I called him an "impulse disorder" (Fenichel, 1945), I was indulging in what Erik Erikson (1964) has aptly termed "diagnostic name-calling." I had known for some time that when I or any other mental health professional stereotypes patients by assigning diagnostic labels to them, we are often using these labels to discharge latent resentment toward them. For example, I have yet to hear a therapist talk positively about a patient who is labelled "sociopathic," "ambulatory schizophrenic," "borderline," or "impulse disorder." As Fine (1982) suggests, when these diagnostic labels are used, they are almost always a sign that a negative countertransference is at work in the clinician.

Although I had only limited difficulty accepting my negative countertransference reactions toward Bob Williams, and although I recovered some childhood and adolescent memories which involved my feeling angry because I was working overtime at home and at school without sufficient appreciation from parents and others, my countertransference reactions toward Bob also helped me gain some insight into his dynamics. As I have suggested in *Resolving Counterresistances in Psychotherapy* (1993), a countertransference reaction not only tells us something about the therapist, but also it can inform us about some hidden dynamics in the patient. Perhaps Bob had the ability to exploit others the way I felt exploited and induce guilty reactions like those I felt if they do not comply with his wishes? I said to myself, "If I ever do meet with him, I'll have to keep that in mind."

Not surprisingly, Bob Williams waited about 10 days before he called again. With some of the aggressive informality that characterized his first telephone call, Bob said, "Hi, Herb. I know you've been waiting for my call but I've been on a lecture tour out of town most of the time. I just did not have time to get to the phone." Again, I felt some annoyance and again I became suspicious of him. I thought, "How come he was so eager to make an appointment with me if he knew he had to be out of town? Is he really telling the truth? And if he is telling the truth, is he trying to impress me with how busy and famous he is?"

Although I was talking to myself, I had not said anything out loud over the phone after Bob told me he knew I'd been waiting for his call while he had been busy. In response to my silence, Bob said, "Look, I have time now to get together. When can we do it?" To several offered times for consultations, Bob had "previous commitments."

When it appeared that Bob and I could not work out a mutually convenient time, I wondered again about how genuine was his motivation for help. Therefore, I suggested to him that perhaps he could call me in another week or two and we could see if we could get together then. Bob did not welcome my suggestion and said gruffly, "Did you say a minute ago that Tuesday at 4:00 P.M. was a possibility?" "Yes," I told him, " but aren't you already committed then?" Bob answered, "Yes, but I can get my supervisee to switch with another one. I'll see you then."

Despite having been in practice almost three decades prior to meeting Bob Williams, I had not felt as much ambivalence before a consultation. Bob's contemptuousness, manipulativeness, intense narcissism, and powerful exhibitionism induced a wide array of uncomfortable feelings in me—anger, competition, envy, dread, and fear. Just before I met Bob face-to-face, I had the strong feeling that I was getting ready to meet a bully from my childhood, and I was not happy about that.

Ten minutes after the scheduled appointment time, Dr. Bob Williams arrived at my office. I had fantasied him to be a tall, well-dressed, possibly bearded man. Instead, he was a short, stocky fellow about 45 years old who was wearing a torn sweater, dirty dungarees, but expensive beads and an ostentatious ring, and I noticed that he needed a haircut and a shave. I also observed that he was prematurely gray.

Bob made no reference to his lateness but immediately launched into a discussion about his recent lecture tour. He informed me that he was "an expert" on short-term therapy and during the last 10 days or so he had visited various treatment centers and led professional groups composed of psychologists and social workers. Bob lectured to them on "strategies" to make treatment "really work after only six to 10 sessions with the patient." Although he had his doctorate in psychology from a prestigious university, Bob told me, "They didn't teach us anything about short-term work so I had to teach myself and others what they neglected to teach me."

There was a brief silence after Bob engaged in this 10-minute monologue about his lecture tour. Not only was I very aware of his exhibitionism and narcissism, but I noted to myself, "He hasn't said a word about his 'sexual issues.' He's obviously very reluctant to expose himself. If I'm direct with him about that, I doubt if I'll be able to involve him in anything further, inasmuch as his obvious narcissistic defense will be punctured." Yet, I felt that I would do Bob a disservice if I ignored what he mentioned over the phone. "Perhaps," I thought to myself, "I could allude to it gently and see what he does with it. If he goes ahead, fine. If not, it's worthwhile information about how resistant he is to therapy."

I asked Bob, after a 20- to 30-second silence, "Shall we discuss today some of the 'issues' you mentioned to me over the phone?" "Oh," responded Bob casually, "you are curious about that, huh?" Then he asked me, "What would you like to know?" I said to myself, "He's certainly not very eager to tell me much about himself. And, there's a very passive-aggressive quality about him which is quite provocative." I warned myself, "You better monitor your irritation." I then asked Bob, "Is there anything about the sexual issues you discussed over the phone that you'd like to discuss now. If so, I would be interested in listening."

Bob replied, "I hope I don't make you too uncomfortable with what I'm about to tell you. But I'll give you a try. The reason I say 'give you a try' is because I've discussed my story with a whole lot of therapists and they get overwhelmed with shock, envy, competition, and more." When I remained quiet, Bob asked, "Do you think you can take it?" I replied, "I'm not sure. Maybe I'll be the same as your other colleagues. You may want to try me out and we'll evaluate together how I do."

"I like your honesty," said Bob. "Unlike other clinicians," Bob continued, "you don't need to impress me with a bunch of Freudian interpretations about my unconscious resistance." And then Bob sensed that he had been too generous with me and recanted by saying, "At least so far you are okay!"

Inasmuch as my initial countertransference reaction to Bob was that I was going to meet with a big bully from my childhood, and therefore felt very intimidated by him, it did not surprise me after hearing his "so far you are okay" to find myself saying to myself, "Round one is over."

Bob then moved on to discuss what he continually termed "the issue." By "the issue" he was referring to the fact that wherever he went women would fall passionately in love with him and insist that they go to bed with him. This was true of colleagues, friends, a couple of relatives, waitresses, and, added Bob with some mild reluctance, "Even my supervisees and patients have to go to bed with me and they are quite relentless about it!" Waiting for my response to his dramatic revelation, Bob looked at me intently but was silent. When he saw that I was not going to respond verbally at this time, Bob went on, "I thought it might be a good idea to talk this over with somebody like you and see what I could do about it. I have to do something because when I go home at night, I've had so much sexual activity that I don't have much energy left over for my wife. She's a good woman and I think she may start to feel jealous. You see, I haven't told my wife Mary about this phenomenon in my life because I have to protect her. But night after night I come home bushed and I'm a little concerned that she may begin to feel slighted. But these other women would be so hurt if I ignored their strong need for me."

As I listened to Bob's story, I was very struck by his almost complete absence of overt anxiety and seeming lack of guilt. Here was a man speaking to a professional colleague about his sexual acting out with patients and supervisees and taking almost no responsibility for himself. He presented himself as a passive victim. His women patients and supervisees could not resist him and he was so altruistic, he did not want to deprive them! His extramarital behavior with nonpatients was experienced by him the same way—he was "a sex object" to hungry women. Furthermore, Bob seemed to have rationalized away his fear of being found out by his wife and merely wanted to "protect her" from feeling hurt and uncomfortable. He seemed to have no insight into the fact that he feared sexual contact with his wife.

It did not surprise me that Bob's story had upset the previous therapists he had consulted. I had never met a patient who seemed so full of superego lacunae or lacked so many ego controls; yet, I had worked with hundreds of prisoners in an army stockade as well as other patients in other settings who were labelled "sociopathic" and "psychopathic." But, Bob's weak object relations, low frustration tolerance, and extreme grandiosity made him appear like a unique baby. "Could he respond to treatment with what he dramatically presented so far—no anxiety, no guilt, and little ability to introspect?" I asked myself. Then I added a qualifier to my musings, "Wait awhile. It may be that you hardly know him and he'll show you later that he can work on some things."

With about 10 minutes remaining before our consultation ended, Bob told me again that the practitioners with whom he consulted to discuss "the issue" were either "alarmed, hostile, lecturing, or defensive." I then said, "I guess you are waiting for me to react similarly." Bob laughed but with an added note of seriousness said, "I'm surprised you haven't lost your cool yet!" "You seem all set to be berated," I observed. To this Bob said, "I guess there are very few men who have been in my position. There is something about my psychodynamics which turns on a diverse group of women. Just this morning, for example, I was with a patient for only the second time. I made a few soothing remarks and before you knew it, she got very excited and she couldn't take 'no' for an answer and so we were at it."

I suggested to Bob that perhaps it might be worthwhile to talk some more about "the issue." In contrast to our phone encounters, Bob and I were able to make the next appointment with relative ease.

I saw Bob for our second interview a week after our first one. During that week I found myself thinking a great deal about him. This obsessing about him was also what happened after our phone calls. He was having a big impact on me and two rather important insights evolved as I reflected about him. As I reviewed Bob's manner of presenting his sexual adventures, not only did I sense a very compulsive quality about them, actually close to an addictive quality, but he sounded much like an ambivalent virgin woman, feeling that she had to submit to an aggressive man. I wondered if Bob were ever placed in this position psychologically when he was a young boy. I also reminded myself that I had previously experienced him as an intrusive and aggressive bully. Pehaps he was bullied as a youngster and then when he was under stress he used the defense that Anna Freud (1946) called "identification with the aggressor."

As I thought some more about Bob's seeming passivity in his sexual relationships and how much he sounded like a reluctant virgin woman, I thought that perhaps his compulsive sexuality and intermittent belligerence defended against strong but unconscious homosexual fantasies.

The other insight that evolved before our second interview was why Bob had upset many therapists, including myself. What most of us repress, Bob was acting out and this I now reminded myself is the difference between an individual suffering from a psychoneurosis and one who is suffering from a perversion. In the case of neurosis, repressed fantasy finds expression only in the form of an ego-dystonic, neurotic symptom. In perversion, a repressed fantasy is capable of becoming conscious and remaining ego-syntonic and pleasurable (Sachs, 1991). Most therapists are inclined to be neurotic and to keep their sexual fantasies under repression. Inasmuch as they can become anxious when they get in touch with their sexual fantasies, when Bob acted out the sexual fantasies that the therapists who interviewed him repress, he made them acutely anxious. I told myself that this was something I had to keep very much in mind if I continued to work with Bob.

At our second interview, Bob began it the same way he began the first, which was to tell me about his lecturing activities. In discussing his expertise in practicing and teaching short-term treatment, it became clear that Bob was not only flexing his therapeutic muscles, but he was challenging me as well. "I know you believe in long-term Freudian stuff," confidently averred Bob. When I did not respond to Bob's provocative remarks about short-term versus long-term treatment, he tried harder. "Are you going to keep me here for years?" I recognized that he was worried about being held down and controlled by me, perhaps sexually exploited (?) and I had to relate to this resistance immediately or there was a chance Bob could bolt. Therefore I asked, "Are you worried that you can't be the decision-maker about your own treatment?" Clearly relieved that I understood him, Bob said, "I'm glad you let your patients write their own tickets. That's what I do in my practice. It's the best way to do it."

When I saw that Bob was terrified of being subdued by me and "held down" for many years, I became more certain that he was constantly coping with strong, passive wishes that he was unconsciously gratifying as he felt eagerly sought after by the women in his life.

In order to unearth some of the historical features of Bob's life, I had to work without threatening him too much as a rigid "long-term Freudian." I asked Bob if he found that during his childhood and teenage years women were very attracted to him and vigorously pursuing him as they were now. "Yes!" declared Bob with certainty and enthusiasm, launching into a discussion of his history, which was equally eventful as his current life.

Bob was the only child of two very unstable alcoholic parents. His father was a taxicab driver who worked intermittently. He was extremely sadistic with Bob, often hitting him and beating him severely, without much, if any, provocation from Bob. For weeks at a time, Bob and his father did not talk to each other. Bob felt that to be with his father, he always ran the risk of being physically or emotionally "destroyed."

Bob's parents had a very poor marital relationship. They frequently argued, hit each other, and often took turns leaving the home. Although one of Bob's parents usually was in the house, occasionally he had to fend for himself with both of them gone.

Bob's mother worked, as a hostess at a nightclub, a little more consistently than his father did. She alternated between being very punitive toward Bob, yelling, screaming, and hitting him, and then would be very loving and physical, hugging him intensely and telling him he was "the best guy" she ever knew. This kind of interaction between mother and son went on from the time Bob was three years old until he was about 16. Frequently, they slept in the same bed, particularly when his mother was drunk.

Bob's father died when Bob was 17 years old. Then, mother and son became closer and spent many hours together—talking intimately, drinking, and in many ways appearing like lovers. When Bob reached age 19 and was in college, he commuted from the family's apartment in the Bronx where he had lived all of his life. At this time he began to find his mother's dependence on him too engulfing and demanding. He started to date young women and this immediately alienated his mother. She constantly demeaned his girlfriends and was castrating toward Bob. Mother began to drink even more and when Bob was 21, his mother died of a liver disorder.

After I listened carefully to Bob's history, and reflected on it, his antisocial behavior became much more understandable to me and I found much of my hostility toward him dissipating. Such as many individuals who have been diagnosed as psychopaths and are "peculiarly intolerant of frustration, inclined to sexual excess, selfish and egotistical, with an immediately ineffective reality sense. . .callous, inconsiderate, unprincipled and lacking in moral sense, incapable of deep attachments, recidivist and refractory to punishment" (Glover, 1960, p. 128), Bob had been emotionally neglected and abandoned (Bowlby, 1951; Gaylin, 1976).

Also similar to most patients diagnosed as sociopathic or psychopathic, Bob later told me he experienced his parents as "brutal." Rather than actively oppose them, he introjected their punitive voices into his superego. The more hatred he felt toward them, the more retaliation he expected, and the more he became subject to a punitive, primitive, and sadistic super-ego. Glover describes this phenomenon as follows:

> The child, projecting his hostile fantasies onto the imagos of the parents, creates imagos that are more powerful and draconic in morality than the parents actually are. . . . As he continues to introject parental imagos, the child intro-jects these distorted elements also, with the result that his unconscious conscience can be more severe (sadistic). . . than are the realistic inferences of the parents. (1960, p. 142)

In contrast to the child who has had empathetic parents that have been able to provide the youngster with optimal matura-tional experiences and which have yielded what Schafer (1960) has called "the loving and beloved superego," Bob and individuals similar to him have an extremely sadistic superego which constantly condemns them.

It was while I was working with Bob that I wrote the following passage in a chapter of my book *Controversy in Psychotherapy* (1982) called "The Psychopath Revisited."

> The psychopath may be described as an individual who is at war with a strong, sadistic, primitive superego that constantly dominates him. He is similar to the child who feels overpowered by aggressively demanding parents and wants to rebel against their strict and punitive controls.

His asocial, aggressive, callous, and impulsive behavior may be viewed as a defensive operation, that is, a rebellion against his punitive superego which he projects onto spouse, family, colleagues, and society in general. Because the psychopath has an unloving superego, he feels that he must be punished for his antisocial activity and that is why he inevitably leaves traces of his misdeeds available for others to see. (p. 259)

It took Bob and me about three sessions to review the major features of his history. When we neared the completion of that task, Bob remarked, "Well I think you've seduced me into coming into treatment with you." Knowing now that he had strong wishes to passively submit sexually but needed to defend against his sexual wishes, it was important to relate to his transference reaction of being "seduced" into treatment. It also was apparent that just as he had projected onto women his wish to seduce them—it was they who were doing the seducing—he had me doing the same. Consequently I asked Bob, "Is that the way it feels, that I'm seducing you into treatment?" A little embarrassed, Bob responded insightfully, "I guess it's difficult for me to say I would like to go ahead with the process." He told me that his current difficulty with me reminded him of when he got married to Mary eight years ago, when he was 35. "She seduced me into marriage and I think she'd like to seduce me into having a baby with her," remarked Bob. He added, "I'm so busy trying to please the other person that I don't get to consider what I want."

THE BEGINNING OF TREATMENT

Bob's resistance to facing his need for therapy together with his strong reluctance to ask for it was not only recapitulated in how his marriage began but it was typical of his manner of relating in most interpersonal situations. With this in mind, I thought it would be helpful to Bob to explore in depth the dynamic meaning of his reluctance to say he wanted treatment. I asked him, "What is it about asking for something like my help that induces discomfort in you?" Bob had a long answer to my question. In fact, a good part of his entire treatment was an attempt to understand his powerful fear of asserting his wishes to be nurtured. For about four sessions of what began as weekly therapy, Bob recalled many memories in which asking for help and/or being dependent on another individual aroused enormous discomfort in him. He talked a great deal about both of his parents who were experienced by him as "untrustworthy." Said Bob, "If you have a father who gets drunk all of the time and beats you most of the time, and a mother who is also a drunk and is full of rage at you, too, you get rather callous. I also learned early in life that people are very selfish. My mother used me too much as a substitute husband and my father used me too much as a whipping boy."

Bob also described how "lonely" he had been most of his life and had spent a good part of time alone and depressed. He rarely had a relationship with anyone he could call a friend. Stated Bob, "I guess what has given me some feeling of self-esteem is that women have always found me to be sexy and sensuous." As if becoming aware, however dimly, that his sexual escapades gave *him* some gratification, Bob altered his emphasis and said, "I've always had to take care of everybody—mother, father, women, and patients."

After Bob had been coming to see me for about three months and had been filling the sessions primarily with painful memories, I felt that inasmuch as he had a lot to say and seemed to find the sessions worthwhile, I asked him how he felt about our getting together twice a week. Bob, at first, seemed to welcome the idea, but when we began to arrange for a second weekly appointment, he talked about all of his commitments that were in his way. And, to confirm my hypothesis that an internal resistance was at work, Bob commented, "I guess I won't be able to give you what you want."

I commented to Bob, "Although I could seduce you into

coming into treatment with me, I can't seduce you to please me some more and come and see me twice a week." In response to my comment, Bob initially laughed and said, "You really know what's going on!" However, as he reflected on the idea that I understood him and wanted to help him, he became very angry with me.

Bob's anger at this point in our work was relentless and intense. "I can't stand somebody who thinks he knows what's right for people!" he bellowed. "You goddamn Freudians who believe in this intensive long-term junk are a bunch of psychopaths." Then looking at me with much disdain, derision, and disgust, and waving his hands, he went on to talk nonstop, virtually yelling at me, and said, "You really don't know what you are doing! You could take a few lessons from me! In one session, I can accomplish more than you can in a year! You are too stuffy and cold to hug, or kiss, or god forbid, go to bed with your patients! You want, instead, to mentally masturbate them and talk about fantasies, dreams, memories, and all that shit! Strean, the day you get me to come here more than once a week and lie on that fucking couch is the day that either I die or you do!"

Although I was somewhat uncomfortable hearing Bob's vituperative remarks, I also felt a certain pleasure. He was bringing out his fundamental distrust of me and of anybody else who got close to him. He was showing me how vulnerable and hateful he had felt with his parents and subsequently with those individuals who would dare come close to him. And, he also revealed to me some dim awareness of his own psychopathy by projecting it onto me and "all the goddamn Freudians." Finally, Bob's enormous fear of his passivity and his homosexuality became ever so clear by his averring that he would rather have one of us die than to lie on a couch. By telling me I would never hug or kiss a patient, he was not only criticizing my rigidity, but he was reassuring himself that I would not come near him physically.

Bob's hostility toward me did not abate for many months. He used almost all of his sessions to attack me, to demean Freudian therapists, and to brag about his own professional competence. In the sessions, most of the time I felt as if I were a nonperson who served no function in Bob's life. Although he arrived on time for his appointments, he rarely greeted me and never even looked at me when we met to start a session. During the sessions, while gazing at the walls or ceiling, he gave eloquent albeit hostile lectures in my office. Once or twice I had the fantasy that at the end of the month he was going to present a bill to me and ask me to pay for listening to his lectures while I was giving him very little.

What took me some time to appreciate was the fact that I was serving as an excellent audience to Bob. I did not question him or threaten him. I did not retaliate when he attacked me and I did not argue with him when he persistently demeaned my point of view about psychotherapy. I also recognized, eventually, that the rage he was cathecting in my direction was a rage that was never consciously felt toward his parents and needed expression.

Despite my eventual realization that I was doing Bob some good, I kept reminding myself of how much Bob left out of the therapy sessions. In coming to his treatment sessions only once a week and spending most of his time angrily lecturing, he did not talk about his marriage at all, avoided examination of his extramarital affairs, and strongly defended his practice of sexually exploiting his patients. His dreams and fantasies were never presented.

As I thought further about all of the pertinent data that Bob was omitting from the treatment sessions, and as I kept observing how frequently I felt ignored by him, it dawned on me how much Bob must have felt ignored in his relationships with significant people in his life. Why would he exclude me and others so much from his life?

After having worked with Bob for a little more than a year, I thought I would raise the aforementioned issue with him. In the middle of a session during the thirteenth month, I interrupted one of Bob's monologues and asked him, "Did you feel constantly excluded in any of your relationships in your past or in the present?" Seeming surprised that I interrupted him and that I was doing some of the talking, Bob in the manner typical of a cold, distant therapist queried, "Why do you ask?" I responded by saying, "Most of the time you want nothing much to do with me. I wonder if you were ever treated that way?"

Just as I surprised Bob with my question, he surprised me with his response. Pausing for a moment, he tearfully exclaimed, "I never felt anybody really cared too much about me and I guess I've had to protect myself. As you know, my parents weren't available to me and I've had to take care of myself. Sometimes I feel Mary is a good wife, but I don't feel too comfortable about letting her into my life. I guess that's what you're saying happens with you. It's a big risk."

A POSITIVE TRANSFERENCE EMERGES

After berating me for over a year, Bob rather dramatically shifted his position and formed an essentially positive transference. He told me that he did not know how I survived the expression of all his hatred, but now that I had, he could begin to like me "a bit." To demonstrate the decline of his malice, he told me he was reading some of my articles and books and was "experimenting" with some of my treatment techniques.

As I listened carefully to Bob's "experiments," it became quite clear that he was now using procedures with his patients that I used with him which he experienced as helpful. With some enthusiasm, he said, "I do a lot less talking now and much more listening. I do a lot less reassuring and let the problems come out. I used to argue much more. I do a lot less of that."

Around the time of his eighteenth month in treatment while Bob was telling me that he and his patients were feeling much more "sympatico" with each other than ever before, he made what appeared to be something like a confession. He confided that he was also experimenting with seeing patients twice a week. Although I immediately hypothesized that Bob was indirectly referring to the possibility of increasing the frequency of his own treatment, I had to be cautious. I knew that when I asked him several months before about seeing me more often, he became extremely paranoid and experienced the equivalent of a homosexual panic. Consequently, it was important that I try not to appear like "the seducer" whom he felt was trying to "manipulate" him. I told myself that if Bob thought about increasing the number of times per week that he saw me, the idea would have to come from him.

However, I did ask Bob how his patients were responding to seeing him more often. He told me he had "chosen the right ones." The "right ones" according to Bob were "the more dependent, less autonomous, and more disturbed" patients. With this response to my question, I realized that Bob was still quite frightened of increased contact with me. If he were to increase the frequency of his sessions, he would worry about experiencing himself and having me experience him as "more dependent, less autonomous, and more disturbed," all pejorative descriptions.

Although Bob was indirectly revealing his own anxieties about intimacy as he talked about his patients, he was enjoying the discussion because he felt more like a colleague than a patient with me. While reflecting on the type of patient he had been seeing more than once a week in treatment, he mentioned that he was also "experimenting" with the idea of "varying his approach." He was now seeing some patients longer than he had previously done, which in his short-term therapy had been for about 12 sessions.

Bob was clearly telling me that he could stand more intimacy with his patients and by implication was able to tolerate more intimacy with me. However, he was still being very wary about seeing me more often and did not directly bring the subject up for another two months. Instead he talked about another therapeutic issue—the gender of the therapist. He pointed out that although a number of therapists took the position that the gender of the practitioner did not make a difference in the therapy, he was of the opinion that it was "a sine qua non." He told me about male patients who needed a father figure because they did not have the benefit of "a warm paternal figure" and that women patients needed a father figure "to feel like a lovable woman." According to Bob, "all of the literature says otherwise."

As I listened to Bob's notions about the gender of the therapist, I had several associations. First, I thought he was indirectly alluding to some of his feelings about my gender. In some ways he liked the idea of my being a man—it gave him someone with whom to identify and supported some of his own masculine strivings. But I thought he was also bothered by my being a man in that it activated his wishes and anxiety about being "a lovable woman." His rigidity on the subject of gender suggested that he was coping with a lot of anxiety about this issue. In his characteristic fashion he projected some of his distortions onto "the literature" and took the mistaken position that the writers on the subject were in agreement and were uniformly neutral.

In addition to pondering the transference implications of Bob's remarks on the gender of the therapist, I was experiencing a new countertransference reaction. I had a fantasy of sharing with him some of the literature on the subject of gender in therapy with which I was familiar. I even thought specifically of telling Bob about Person's articles (1983, 1985) that dealt with "therapist gender as a variable." As I analyzed my fantasy, I realized that I was trying to make Bob a colleague and share ideas with him, something I wondered about when he called me for the first time at my home almost two years before. However, my fantasy revealed that I also wanted to supervise him and correct some of his misunderstandings.

Inasmuch as I had been convinced for some time that countertransference reactions always give some clue as to what is currently transpiring in the patient's transference fantasies (Strean, 1993), it did not surprise me too much that when I was starting to feel closer to Bob and wanted him to be a colleague and/or a supervisee, he returned to a discussion of frequency of visits. Bob pointed out that different patients experience the frequency of treatment quite differently. Bob said, "Some patients see it as an opportunity to form a stronger therapeutic alliance. Some see it as an opportunity to learn more. Some see it as a way to improve faster."

I now felt that Bob was being less critical of himself about wanting more from me. In effect he was implying that he could learn more, improve faster, and use me more as a resource. However, I felt that interpreting this to him would increase his anxiety rather than diminish it. Therefore, I said nothing.

It was exactly two years to the day that Bob had been in treatment when he asked me in the session, "When a patient mentions coming more often, do you always encourage the idea?" I knew I was being tested here and with Bob's mixed feelings in mind I replied, "Oh no. I try to explore the patient's mixed feelings and always leave the decision up to him or her." Bob said he did the same with his patients. Then, after a silence of about 20 seconds, he remarked, "I've been giving the idea some thought and I might want to come here more often."

To Bob's last statement, I remarked, "Oh?" and then Bob burst out laughing, saying, "Herb Strean, you practice what you preach! You are not going to talk me into this. Bravo. Touché."

Bob was reassured by my approach and therefore became less frightened to be involved with me. I wondered though about his associations to "touché"; did he worry about touching or being touched? The answer to this question had to wait. Nonetheless, after talking about schedules and hearing me say, "There was no rush" and "Maybe you'd like to talk about the plusses and minuses some more," Bob, after two years and three weeks with me, started to see me twice a week.

THE TREATMENT BECOMES MORE INTENSIVE

After he began to see me more frequently, Bob started to report fantasies and dreams. Most of them involved his being a little child, having me fondle him for awhile, and then abruptly all contact would cease. At first these dreams and fantasies took a disguised form in their manifest content. The child in the dream was a youngster from Bob's past or one that he had treated in child therapy. The therapist in the dreams and fantasies was either himself or another adult. Gradually Bob could see that he was talking about himself and me, after which the dreams and fantasies became more direct and distinct.

Bob shared with me that he had never really talked about dreams or fantasies with previous therapists. He also confided that he had wanted to appear to me as if he had more personal therapy than he really did. Actually Bob had never been in any sustained treatment. He had participated in a couple of therapeutic groups but found the group members to be "too paranoid" and "too argumentative." In his individual contacts with practitioners, he found them to be "too ingratiating" and/or "too supportive." No treatment lasted over six months.

I could now see clearly why Bob was a staunch supporter and firm believer in brief treatment. Not only did it help Bob stay away from deep and intimate relationships, which he feared, but he was not able to offer his patients something that he had not experienced. He could take his patients only as far as he had travelled in his personal treatment and that was not very far.

During Bob's twenty-sixth month of treatment he reported a dream in which he was a little boy crawling toward me and just as I was about to pick him up and put him on my lap, Bob woke up in terror. When Bob had difficulty associating to his dream, I asked him, "What is terrifying about being my little boy and being held?" Tearfully, and with some desperation his voice, Bob said that if he permitted himself to regress and feel like my little boy, he would remain permanently regressed and act out childish impulses "from now to doomsday."

When I asked Bob what childish wishes he was afraid to act out with me, just like in his dream, he abruptly turned away from the subject. I commented on this, recognizing with Bob that he was so terrified of his fantasies that he always felt compelled to look away from them. I asked him what the danger was if we talked about what he wanted. After a brief silence, Bob said, "I guess I'm worried that you and I will do the same thing that I do with my patients—our talk will lead to action."

I felt that Bob and I were at a very important phase in our work. He experienced himself with me the same way that his patients with whom he acted out experienced him. They wanted to gratify childish impulses and Bob literally put them on his lap instead of talking with them about the why's and wherefore's of their sexualized transferences. I wanted to help Bob see that talking could help him.

When I said to Bob that as much as he was uncomfortable with the idea of getting on my lap and having me cuddle him, it was easier than talking about what he thought, felt, and remembered when he had the wish to do so. Somewhat irritated with me now, Bob said, "Oh, you want to get me to talk about how I'd like to suck your cock, fuck you up the ass, have you do the same to me and all that stuff. And, you probably want me to acknowledge out loud that I'd like to be your little girl, too. Yeah, I know what you want!"

I interpreted to Bob that, just like with his patients and others as well, when a relationship became close, he was convinced he had to "put out" for the other person and "be violated."

Bob then had an insight that was both profound and helpful to him. He remarked, "I know you want me to talk about what I feel and not do anything else here. It's because I hate to give you what you want that makes me try to do something very different. By the way, when I act on my feelings with my patients, I'm telling you and the whole therapeutic establishment to go to hell! I want to do it my way!"

Bob and I were eventually able to link his rebelliousness toward me and "the therapeutic establishment" to his rage at both his parents. Referring to them, Bob angrily asked, "Why should I give them what they want? Did they ever feed me properly? Why should I give them the satisfaction of getting their needs met when they never did anything for me?"

I interpreted to Bob that in many ways he was experiencing me as if I were both his mother and father. I remarked, "You don't want to talk with me because I've said that's what I would like from you—to talk. You want to deprive me because I've deprived you." I then asked, "What do you want that I have not given you?"

After a moment of hesitation, Bob mentioned a number of things that I had not given to him and pointed out that my "depriving attitude" had "infuriated" him. He stated that I was "much too much of a Freudian analyst" who was "extremely withholding." Combining tones of both belligerence and sadness, Bob admonished me saying, "You rarely smile at me. You've never shaken my hand. You would never put your arm around me. Not once have you invited me to your psychoanalytic institute to give a paper, teach a class, or participate in a discussion! Wouldn't it be nice to ask me to write a paper with you? But, you wouldn't do that. You'd rather be a pure technician than a warm human being. Don't you think it would be a kind gesture to buy me a cup of coffee? Why haven't you ever asked me over to your house? You withhold, you withdraw, you deprive!"

In his most direct and clearest language to date, Bob was telling me how exasperated he was with me because I had not taken him into my family, made him my son, and loved him the way he wanted his mother and father to love him. The rage, hurt, and keen disappointment he was expressing were feelings he had harbored much of his life.

I very much wanted to help Bob discuss the intense feelings he had repressed and suppressed for many years. Yet, whenever Bob thought there was something he could do that would be helpful to his therapy, he would try his best to defeat it. Consequently, I shared my dilemma with him. "Bob," I said, "what you've been talking about seems very central to your life and to our work. If I encourage you to talk about it, and you do, how much of a favor do you think you'll be doing for me?"

Initially, Bob laughed when he heard my question. But, with some seriousness in his voice, he asked, "Have I always been trying to defeat you?" When I did not say anything, but nonverbally implied that he try to answer the question, Bob said, "I'm becoming aware of how much I've been trying to displease and oppose you. But I feel a lot better these days and I don't have to fight you as much." He then went on to tell me that from the beginning of our contact he had fantasies of being my son and "growing from the experience." Bob confided that he always "craved" my attention, yearned to hear me laugh, and wanted to put his head in my lap and cry "to get out all of the tears of sadness that have been stored up for many years."

As Bob discussed at length what he wanted from me, how hurt he was in not receiving it, he also brought in more memories from his childhood. In each childhood vignette, he was ignored, frustrated, or demeaned. He continued to deplore his fate, lamenting again that he was hardly ever embraced, touched, or kissed by anyone. As he reported how hungry he still was for physical contact, he began to fill me in on the details of his sexual liaisons with his patients.

THE DYNAMICS OF BOB'S SEXUAL AFFAIRS
WITH PATIENTS

Because Bob and I had focused a great deal on how hungry he was for physical contact, particularly how much he wanted me to embrace him, hug him, and fondle him, he was able to tell himself and me with much clarity just what his central motives had been that provoked his actual physical contacts with patients.

Although at times it took the form of a didactic lecture, Bob was able nonetheless to articulate in his treatment sessions what specific neurotic problems of his activated his sexual exploitation of patients. What Bob became keenly aware of was why he "kept patients" in treatment with him for only a short period of time. Stated Bob, "I guess I have not wanted to see too much of their neediness, so I've given them what I thought they wanted from me and then told them to leave."

Not only did Bob not want to face his patients' "neediness" because it would remind him too much of his own, but as he himself insightfully pointed out, "I think I abandoned them the same way I've been abandoned." In so doing, Bob displaced the rage he felt toward parental figures onto his patients. He had them suffer the way he suffered – an identification with the aggressor (A. Freud, 1946).

What I eventually learned from Bob was that most of his sexual contacts with patients were forms of pregenital sex. There was a great deal of kissing, hugging, fellatio, cunnilingus, but almost no instances of coitus. When I asked Bob why he avoided sexual intercourse with his patients, at first he gave me a rather perfunctory and moralistic response, saying, "Direct sex might interfere with the therapy. Hugging, kissing, and touching, I felt, are for the patients and are therapeutic. Screwing would be for me."

When I remained silent as Bob tried to rationalize his fear of coitus, it did not take him long to explore his inhibitions openly. He began to fantasy about the vagina and told me, "When I'm in a woman, she appears so big to me and I feel so small. I'm afraid she'll eat me up or castrate me. That's why I stay out." Bob's fear of the vagina and his "staying out" of it also was a factor in his having only short-term affairs with patients and nonpatients. He eventually saw how much he had to protect himself from being enveloped by a woman and the best way was "to have only limited contact."

In discussing and analyzing Bob's sexual contacts with patients and nonpatients, what became increasingly clear was how much hatred he was expressing – toward his parents, his therapists, and his patients. The hatred toward his patients was overdetermined. Not only did he hate them because they appeared to be "big mamas" who could weaken and castrate him, but also he projected his own weak self-image onto them and would rather be contemptuous of them than confront his own self-loathing. It was as if he were saying to his women patients, "You are a weak, despicable woman, not I!"

Hull, Lane and Okie (1989) in their paper, "Sexual Acting Out and the Desire for Revenge," suggest that patients act out sexually when an internalized relationship with an exciting but frustrating object has been activated in the transference. The authors' following statement seems pertinent to Bob.

Because of past deprivations and losses the patient expects to be abandoned or denied at the moment of closeness with the analyst, when gratification finally seems within reach. Sexual acting out is likely to follow these moments of closeness, because of the patient's intense excitement and strong expectations of renewed frustration. . . . Multiple purposes and functions may be identified, but the primary motive usually is to get revenge against the analyst and other objects for present and past disappointments. (p. 317)

When we consider Bob's extreme and pervasive sexual acting out, Freud's (1914) explanation of acting out also seems very pertinent. Freud saw acting out as behavior that emerges in the place of verbal recall, a resistance to remembering childhood conflicts. Because Bob's childhood conflicts were so painful to him, he repressed them and did not want to talk about them. Hence, acting out seemed to be the only outlet for him.

Grinberg (1968) describes acting out as a phenomenon that always involves two participants and is related to experiences of unresolved problems of separation and loss. Extending Bion's (1962) idea that a young infant who experiences intense anxiety needs to find "a container" capable of holding the anxiety, Grinberg stresses that the acting-out patient has a need to find an object in the external world that contains the patient's separation anxiety, an object into which feelings can be "evacuated."

What Blum (1973) has written about the "eroticized transference" in patients who seek revenge and reparation for past object losses through seduction of the analyst could be transposed to the therapist. Clinicians who act out sexually with their patients may also be seeking reparation for past losses. This was certainly true of Bob Williams.

BOB LOOKS AT HIS MARRIAGE

It was not until late in Bob's third year of therapy that he began to examine in more detail his relationship with his wife. Mary, an elementary schoolteacher, was consistently described by Bob as a "kind" woman. Despite her warmth and concern for Bob, he frequently demeaned and was contemptuous of her.

As we explored Bob's continuous disparagement of Mary, we learned that he was very sadistic toward her when he became aware of her vulnerabilities. As with his patients, Bob attacked Mary when she appeared lacking in confidence, showed dependence on him or others, or was indecisive. These were characteristics that he could not tolerate in himself. Consequently he projected his own limitations and vulnerabilities onto Mary and attacked her instead of confronting himself.

Bob rarely initiated sex with Mary. Although he rationalized his sexual inhibitions with his wife by talking about her "lack of passion," further exploration revealed that Bob had unconsciously turned Mary into a mother figure and avoided her sexually. Again, as with his patients, in bed with Mary Bob felt like a little boy being enveloped by a mother who would eventually castrate him.

In discussing his marriage, Bob realized that many of his fears and anxieties that emerged were virtually identical to those we had discussed earlier when we examined his relationships with his female patients. Because Bob was beginning to feel more like a male adult with his patients as a result of understanding himself better, he rather easily moved into a more constructive, cooperative relationship with Mary. As he made her less of "a big mama" and made himself less of a little boy, sexual relations with Mary became more frequent and more mutually enjoyable. Toward the end of Bob's fourth year of treatment, Mary gave birth to a son which brought Mary and Bob even closer. Bob was extremely responsive to his young son and many times voiced the conviction, "He'll get a lot more from his parents than I did."

TERMINATION OF TREATMENT

With the birth of a baby, his marriage going quite well, and his sexual exploitation of patients having ceased, Bob thought it would be a good idea to consider ending the treatment. Although he had made considerable progress, I thought Bob had more therapeutic work to do. I believed his strong, infantile wishes needed more expression, particularly his strong oral dependency. I also thought he still had some unresolved rage that needed to be explored in treatment. I had hoped that he would use the couch, come to see me three or four times a week, face unexplored areas of his unconscious, and grow further.

Despite my wanting to work with Bob longer, I knew him well enough to realize that pressure and persuasion from me or anyone else only alienated him. I also knew that for a man who championed short-term relationships in both his personal and professional contacts, staying with me for over four years was an achievement with which I should have been satisfied. Above all, I knew the worst thing I could do would be to get into an argument with Bob and try to cajole him to stay in treatment.

As he discussed termination, Bob, typical of most patients, regressed (Firestein, 1978). He began to feel that I was appearing like a warden who was keeping him in prison. Despite the fact that I had remained completely neutral about Bob's decision, he was sure I would try to make him stay in treatment with me "indefinitely." He went on a tirade, telling me that I fostered long-term relationships in therapy because I enjoyed "exploiting" my patients and "wanted their money." He was sure I was trying "to put [him] into a deep analysis and convert [him] to [my] rigid Freudian point of view." Although there was reality to some of Bob's accusations, I had to keep in mind that the gentleman was protesting much too much.

When Bob saw that I did not argue with him about any of his accusations, he became more subdued. He told me that he was quite sure that I would see him again if he wanted to return to treatment after we terminated. However, when he asked me directly if he was correct about the possibility of returning after a hiatus, I suggested to Bob that I had the impression he wasn't quite sure about my attitude. "Yeah," said Bob, "I can't be certain that you aren't angry at me!" I hypothesized out loud that he probably had some fantasies about what he was doing when he terminated treatment that he thought aroused my anger. To validate this point, Bob brought in a dream in which a female policeman was arresting him for speeding in his car and told him if he did not slow down he would be in trouble. Bob was able to interpret most of the dream by himself.

He realized that he was "in too much of a hurry" to leave treatment, that in fact he was speeding, trying to get away from me. By arranging for me to "arrest" him, part of him was trying to get me to stop him. When I asked Bob why he thought he made me a woman police officer in the dream, after struggling a bit he said, "If I stay in treatment with you, I feel like a woman and you are a big man. If I leave, I'll turn you into a woman and I'll be in good shape."

Bob's fear of intimacy with which he came into treatment asserted itself at termination. In effect, he was saying once again that if he relied on another person, unconsciously he would feel like a woman so he had to run. Although Bob could face his desires to be a woman with more equanimity, his dread of the wish was making him flee therapy prematurely. Although we both knew this, Bob felt that he wanted to try it on his own, nonetheless.

I did hear from Bob about one year after treatment had ended. He called me after he had read an article I had written and informed me that his marriage was going well, his son (whom he named after me) was fine, and his practice was productive. Regarding his acting out sexually with his patients, he said, "You have become my superego and I think of you when I am tempted."

ASSESSMENT OF BOB'S THERAPY

Bob moved toward the analytic ideal (Fine, 1982) but his fear of his feminine wishes stopped him from receiving further treatment and maturing as much as I think he could have. Although he loved more and hated less, there were still pockets of unresolved hatred in him. His sexual and interpersonal life with Mary improved markedly, but I thought that with a crisis he could regress. His work life changed dramatically and I felt confident that he would not return to exploiting his patients sexually or in any other way. He was capable of a wider range of feelings than when he began treatment, was much more creative, was a more responsible member of society, and became free of neurotic symptoms. I retained the wish, nonetheless, that Bob would return someday to me or someone else for further psychotherapy.

Chapter V

THE CASE OF AL GREEN

A Sadomasochistic Social Worker Who Makes His Female Ex-patients Suffer

I walked into the waiting room of my office suite and saw a man of about 50 years of age busily pacing the room with his head drooped toward the floor, who appeared extremely preoccupied. His face was pale and his baggy trousers and mismatched jacket that had several stains on it gave me the instant and strong impression that this man was quite depressed. I greeted him saying, "Hi, I'm Dr. Strean." In a low and expressionless voice, he meekly, almost apologetically, responded, "Hello, I'm Mr. Green."

I invited Mr. Green into my office, pointed to the chair where he could sit, and I then sat down in a chair facing him. After a silence of about 10 seconds, I asked Mr. Green if he could tell me what brought him to see me. "I'm a social worker at the Brookside Mental Health Center* and I also have a small private practice. One of the social workers at the Center, my supervisor, said I needed therapy. So that's why I called you for an appointment," stated Mr. Green, in a low monotone voice, conspicuous for its absence of affect.

As I listened to Mr. Green's introduction of himself, I found my initial impression of him in the waiting room corroborated. I remarked to myself, "There are very few men of his age in social work working under supervision in a clinic and with only

*a pseudonymous title

a small private practice. This guy sounds and looks like a loser. I wonder if he is."

Just a little bit later in the interview, I silently wondered if Mr. Green wanted therapy for himself or whether he was an involuntary patient, merely acceding to his supervisor's pronouncement. I thought I would ask him about this. "Are you here because you would like to be a cooperative supervisee or do you have reasons of your own to get some therapy?" Mr. Green responded, "My supervisor is right. I need more therapy."

After another silence of approximately 30 seconds, I asked Mr. Green, "Is it difficult to tell me your thoughts about getting more therapy?" In a still lower voice than the one I noted earlier, and with extremely depressed affect, he answered, "A lot of the patients I see in treatment quit. I lose a lot in my private work, too. My supervisor told me that I overidentify excessively with them, talk too much, gratify them too much, don't know how to frustrate them, and don't know how to use limits."

When I did not overtly respond to his quoting his supervisor's disparaging remarks about him, Al Green found more ammunition to knock himself. He next told me that the executuve director of the Brookside Center suggested to him that he was "self-abnegating," but Al Green "wasn't sure what that meant."

After I had been with him for about 15 minutes, Al Green reminded me of many children I had seen in treatment who in their first interview would spend a great deal of time telling me how their parents, teachers, or other adults wanted them to be in therapy and how these individuals justified their recommendation. Just as it was crucial in helping these children to discuss in breadth and depth how they felt toward those individuals who had recommended treatment for them, it was important for me to ask this question of Al Green. When I did ask him, he told me, "I think my supervisor has a right to have her opinion about me. I don't do good work and I think I should be helped to do better. The executive director of the center agrees."

It was becoming increasingly clear that Al Green had quite a bit of latent resentment about being referred to me and that if

I was going to help him at all, I had to address this issue with him. Therefore I said to Al, "As you know from your own work, nobody can get much out of a therapy experience by obeying someone else. I really wonder if you feel compelled to comply with your supervisor's suggestion?" He replied, "Look, everywhere I go I manage to screw up. I do lousy work at the Center and with my private patients. I don't get along with the staff members; they think I'm not friendly. This has been true of all my jobs. I also don't have any friends to speak of. My marriage is bad. My wife keeps telling me I'm a weak, sad sack. Even my 14-year-old daughter thinks I'm a jerk."

Al Green had not answered my question about his own feelings about treatment, but instead he kept telling me about how he was an abysmal failure in virtually anything and everything he undertook and how he had disappointed many individuals throughout his life. He even took responsibility for making two of his own personal experiences of therapy "a disaster." In one experience with a male therapist, the latter became so "infuriated" with Al for frequently coming late to treatment sessions and for bouncing checks, he threw him out of treatment. In another experience with a female practitioner, his "passivity" and inability to assert himself, particularly in his relationship with his wife, Sharon, made her "give up" on him.

In discussing his history, Al told me he was brought up in a "decrepit" area of the Bronx. He was the youngest of four brothers and was "the family scapegoat." His siblings teased and taunted him throughout his childhood and adolescence and both of his parents "agreed" with his brothers that he was "worthless." Al's mother was the dominant parent who "ruled the Jewish home like all Jewish mothers do." Father was described as a very passive man who spent most of his time driving a taxicab, having little to do with the family.

Al's position in the family was recapitulated in his relationships with peers. Both at school and in the neighborhood, he was "an outsider and a scapegoat." Reminisced Al, "I did not feel close to anyone as a child, teenager, or as an adult. I was never a good student; I never have done anything worthwhile.

I graduated high school by the skin of my teeth. I think they made a mistake in letting me graduate from college. My average was very low. I almost flunked out of school of social work."

Toward the end of the interview, after Al had clearly demonstrated that he had been an extremely depressed individual most of his life and after telling me that he had experienced intermittent suicidal fantasies for as long as he could remember, he mentioned something about himself that stood out in sharp contrast to all that he had presented until this time. With the only note of enthusiasm that I observed in him in the interview, he remarked, "Although I was always faithful to my wife throughout our marriage of 15 years, during the last two or three years I've had some affairs." When I remained silent but interested, Al went on to tell me, "These affairs have been with three different women – each for a period of about six months. All three were patients I had worked with, but I terminated treatment before the affairs began."

What was impressive about Al's statement was not only his uncharacteristic pleasure when talking about his affairs with these former patients, but equally impressive and also quite surprising was his seeming lack of guilt when he spoke about the liaisons. "All three of these women were married and came to see me for marital problems. Although I did not help them too much with their marriages, when I called them to have a cup of coffee after treatment was over, they were glad to hear from me and glad to see me," said Al with some glee.

All of the women patients with whom Al had sexual liaisons after treatment ended were his private patients. They had sex with him in his office which, Al pointed out, "was quite enjoyable for them and me." As was true with most of Al's relationships, his "patient-lovers eventually became irritated" with him and ended the affairs. They became upset when he "forgot" the times of their "dates" and therefore failed to meet with them as they had planned. They resented him when he did not call them for weeks at a time. Finally, in many conversations, he had nothing much to say to them and they became either bored or exasperated.

Toward the end of the consultation, when I asked Al how often he wished to come to see me, he did not answer directly but instead said, "My two therapists both wanted me to come twice a week, so I saw them twice a week." Smiling, I asked Al, "Are you waiting for me to tell you how frequently you should come to see me?" Al responded, "I guess so" without showing any visible emotional reaction.

Inasmuch as the allotted time for the consultation had elapsed, I suggested to Al that he might want to consider having a say in determining how often he should see me. "Perhaps you might want to make another appointment and we can discuss this some more?" I asked. As I had anticipated, Al agreed with my suggestion and we made another appointment. When I wondered what would be a convenient time for him, Al again tried to make the time and day my decision. I then said, "I'm starting to have the impression that you are very quick to forget about your own needs and think exclusively of the other guy's." "Yeah," replied Al, "my other therapists said the same thing." I then remarked to myself sarcastically, "And a lot of good it has done you!" Out loud I said, "It may be something you would like to look at some more."

After my first consultation with Al, I found myself thinking a great deal about two issues involving him. One was Al's obvious and extreme masochism and the other was his practice of having sexual liaisons with former women patients.

Regarding Al's masochism, I recalled the many pertinent points that my former teacher Theodor Reik (1941) had made in his highly readable and informative book, *Masochism in Modern Man*. Reik pointed out that the extreme suffering that the masochist endures is unconsciously desired. The suffering is aimed to punish the person for real or fantasied misdeeds. Said Reik, "The superego imposes many different penalties: failure in a career, unhappy marriage, misfortunes, and dis-appointments of every kind relating to life and love" (p. 11).

As I reflected further on Al's masochism, I recalled another statement by Reik that seemed pertinent to Al, namely his "silent suffering." Stated Reik, "such conspicuously silent suffering is meant to be seen. The equanimity with which it is borne is meant to be admired" (p. 77).

When I began to analyze why I had been thinking so much about Al's masochism, it dawned on me that one of the reasons was Al's subtle but genuine wish to exhibit himself to me and have me be an attentive audience who takes note of all "the slings and arrows of [his] outrageous fortune." Reik also commented on this dynamic constellation:

> His displaying and showing himself have all the characteristics of wooing, of making himself noticeable. His behavior is just the counterpart to narcissistic behavior. . . . Evidently the narcissism of these masochistic persons had been deeply disturbed as they make such frantic efforts to attract the attention of the other. (p. 82)

Another part of Al's masochism was his "skilled" manner of making constant enemies. Although he presented himself as a victim, I had the distinct impression that inasmuch as he was badly treated in so many of his interpersonal relationships, he had an investment in being exploited. Reik also was conversant with this theme:

> This psychic martyrdom, eager to sacrifice itself, is aimed at a cherished and hated victim, the wife, the parent, the children, a friend. An adverse destiny has been personified. It has saddled the masochist with a grumbling boss, with an eternally sick and nagging wife, ungrateful children, exacting relatives and friends. . . .The secret urge to arouse envy and jealousy, hatred and wrath in others, to create a host of enemies for oneself is part of the provocative technique of social masochism. (p. 89)

In previous work with patients similar to Al, my countertransference reactions had retarded therapeutic progress because I felt too sorry for them. I had not been sufficiently aware of the pleasure these patients derived from their pain.

By showing too much sympathy, I had gratified the neurotic part of these patients that wanted admiration and appreciation for their martyrdom. I told myself that this would be something I would have to monitor carefully in my work with Al.

I also reminded myself of a paradox that I had observed in masochistic patients. Despite the acute humiliation, punishment, degradation, and discomfort they experienced, they were always people who persevered until they achieved what they were looking for. It took me a long time to comprehend that the masochistic person was hardly ever a complete celibate or a full-blown prude. Rather, he or she, in a manner that is not obvious, says repeatedly, "Beat me, punish me, deride me, derogate me. That's always part of the drama I enact until I attain what I'm looking for."

This paradox, I thought, could possibly explain Al's sexual exploitation of his women patients. "Perhaps," I conjectured, "he has a secret sadistic wish to turn his women patients into lovers? Maybe he does not really want to help them but wants to take advantage of them instead. And for this, he is willing to undergo much pain and punishment until he achieves what he deeply desires."

I felt there was probably much revenge in Al's behavior. He upset too many people too often for me to think otherwise. It would be important, I warned myself, to remember what Reik often said to his masochistic patients when they exhibited suffering in their therapy sessions and he wanted them to face their underlying sadism and revenge. Dr. Reik frequently told those of us who were his students that he would periodically say to all of his masochistic patients and advised us to say the same, "No rachmonis!" In Yiddish this means, "No pity."

I told myself more than once between the first and second interviews that by not indulging Al's suffering with my pity, perhaps I could help him face his underlying sadism—the affect that probably sparked his sexual exploitation of patients and, in all likelihood, contributed heavily to his sadomasochistic modus vivendi. In further preparing myself to treat Al Green, I recalled my favorite passage from Reik's *Masochism in Modern*

Man (1941), which I have memorized and quoted several times in books and articles:

> The masochist is a revolutionist of self-surrender. The lambskin he wears hides a wolf. His yielding includes defiance; his submissiveness, opposition. Beneath his softness, there is hardness; behind his obsequiousness, rebellion is concealed. (p. 156)

At the time I began my work with Al Green, all of the major mental health organizations representing social workers, psychiatrists, psychologists, and psychoanalysts had condemned in writing psychotherapists having sexual contact with patients. However, debate raged (and still does) over the ethics of posttermination therapist-patient sexual contact (Appelbaum & Jorgenson, 1991). In a national survey of psychiatrists (Herman, Gartrell, Olarte, Feldstein, & Localio, 1987), approximately one-third of those responding thought that sex with a former patient might be appropriate. Two studies by psychologists (Akamatsa, 1988; Pope, Tabachnik, & Keith-Spiegal, 1987) reflected a similar division of opinion between those who believed that sex after termination of treatment might be acceptable and those who contended it was not. One study of therapists on the faculty of the department of psychiatry of a major medical school (Conte, Plutchik, Picard, & Karasu, 1989) found that only 29.6% of them believed that marrying a patient after psychotherapy was terminated was unethical. In 1988 the American Association for Marriage and Family prescribed that therapists should wait only two years after the termination of treatment before initiating sexual contact.

It would appear that the justifications for preventing sexual contact with clinicians after termination of treatment are much weaker than while treatment is ongoing. In a thorough study of posttermination sexual contact, Appelbaum, a psychiatrist, and Jorgenson (1991), an attorney, concluded their research by advocating a one year interval between termination and sexual contact, contending that the force of transference diminishes when therapist and patient are separated for a period of time. Patients thereby are afforded an opportunity for reflection on their attraction to their therapist and are likely to be free of possible coercive pressures. Therapists, too, are given a substantial period of time to consider the desirability of involvement with the former patients.

Appelbaum and Jorgenson (1991) reject an absolute ban on posttermination sexual contact. They believe "therapists are not parents" and "an absolute ban would preclude relationships that may involve no more problems than many relationships routinely sanctioned in our society" (p. 1466).

Writers who have discussed and researched posttermination sexual contacts between therapists and patients have focused too exclusively on the ethics, morals, legality, and civil rights issues that pertain to the topic. What has been seriously neglected is a discussion of the transference-countertransference fantasies that contribute to the posttermination affair. Furthermore, in dynamic psychotherapy, the goal of treatment is separation between therapist and patient—not reunion. It would appear that when patient and therapist arrange to have sex with each other after termination, certain transference and countertransference issues have been unresolved and are being acted out rather than analyzed and mastered. As we will demonstrate with Al Green, his desire to have affairs with patients was part and parcel of his neurotic countertransference problems toward them, which interfered with his being able to help his patients give up their attachment to him.

AL'S BEGINNING INTERVIEWS

I did not see Al on a regular basis for the first couple of months of my contact with him. Despite his passivity and obsequiousness, he became very insistent that I tell him how often he should see me and when he should come. Inasmuch as he was so controlled and dominated by his previous therapists, I thought it would be important to try to make his contact with me different in this respect. At one point I told Al directly, "I keep having the impression that you have a strong resistance to taking initiative and making decisions. I think it would be helpful for us to see why it's so uncomfortable for you to think out loud about how often you'd like to see me and when you'd like to come."

Al became somewhat irritated with me and said, "You make me feel like I'm a weak dope, deprived of any backbone and a depraved man. Maybe you are right. I don't know how to make decisions. Why don't you help me?" I told Al that I was trying to help him with decision-making by not making the decisions for him, but trying instead to investigate what was in his way from making them himself. He resented my response and gazed at me plaintively but with some scorn.

As I worked with Al on the issue of frequency of appointments, I could feel the same annoyance in myself that his family, friends, colleagues, and patients told Al he had induced in them. I began to realize that Al was trying to provoke me into getting angry at him. "Perhaps," I wondered to myself, "he would derive some masochistic pleasure from my terminating him?"

When Al suggested in his fifth interview that I was being "stubborn," I said to myself, "Regardless of how stubborn I am, he's projecting some of his own stubbornness onto me. See what he says about my stubbornness." I then asked Al, "How does my stubbornness make you feel?" He replied, "You are the first professional I've met who irritates me. You find it difficult to see my problem and you insist that I should resolve it before we understand it. You ask too much from me."

I welcomed Al's expressions of defiance because he was becoming more genuine with me and was showing "the real wolf" behind his thin "lambskin." I told him I thought it would be helpful for our work to tell me about his criticisms of me whenever he felt them. Al looked at me in disbelief but did say, "Well, if it's helpful, I'll do what I did in the past. I'll come and see you twice a week." Then he went on to suggest some dates and times for regular appointments. Although it was clear that

Al's statement reflected a breakthrough of some of his latent resentment toward me and it did free him to move toward making an autonomous decision, he also was showing me something that was part of his stubborn resistance. He wanted to do what he "did in the past" – arrange a set-up with me that was identical to the set-up with therapists who had failed him. When I remarked about this in our seventh interview, Al said, "Let's try it. I'll come twice a week but this time it will be different I think." I respected Al's wishes and began to see him twice a week at regularly scheduled appointments as the third month of our contact began.

FEARS OF ASSERTION

Inasmuch as Al welcomed the opportunity of aggressing toward me and therefore became less depressed, he started coming to his interviews with less tentativeness and with a little more enthusiasm. He recognized how intimidated he had been feeling toward me and how frequently he felt this way in most of his interpersonal relationships. This recognition motivated him to begin to explore his strong fear of his own aggression.

First, Al discussed his conviction that if he did assert himself, the person hearing his remarks would not be interested in him, would laugh at him, or if he or she did not like what Al said, this person would become very punitive. He recalled how true this was in the past with his parents and brothers. "Whenever I objected to anything or even when I just said what was on my mind, they would all gang up on me and yell at me," Al lamented. He went on to say that it was quite similar in his current home, where his wife and daughter frequently scoffed at his remarks. "And, as you know, " added Al, "I get it all the time at the agency whenever I say anything but 'Good morning.'"

When Al contrasted my response to his assertiveness with those of others, contending that I was unique in not being vindictive or retaliatory, I was able to help him see that when he was critical of me, he experienced himself as an adult male, telling an equal what was on his mind. "Most of the time you turn others into powerful parental figures and make yourself a vulnerable child," I remarked.

Al welcomed my interpretation, finding it "mind-boggling" that he had unwittingly been relating to the world as if he were a weak child. Stated Al with conviction, "I feel now for the first time in my life that I have the power to influence my life if I don't believe I have to be the sad sack I was in the Bronx."

During Al's fourth and fifth months of treatment, he brought in many vignettes from work and home, indicating that he was starting to believe he had a right to express his opinions and was not being "little Alan from the Bronx" so much of the time. Al also told me that Sharon and his daughter Becky were showing him more respect as were his colleagues and superiors at the Center.

Although Al reported feeling "liberated" and in a better frame of mind than he had been in many years, I noted that toward the end of the fifth month of treatment, his positive mood began to ebb. He started coming late for sessions, there were many silences in them, and his affect seemed quite depressed again. When I shared these observations and asked him if he noted them, too, Al merely said, "Something is different, but I don't know what it's all about."

When I encouraged Al to explore his dramatic shift in the manner he had been relating to me and further suggested that he try to remember his dreams and tell them to me, Al balked. It was becoming increasingly clear that his transference toward me had shifted to a negative one and this had to be confronted. Therefore, I told Al, "You know from your own work when a patient comes late for sessions and has little to say that he's bothered by the therapist." I then asked him, "What's bothering you about me these days?"

In consonance with his current masochistic and depressed outlook, Al told me that nothing bothered him about me, he was just a very resistant patient who "may be too sick to get better." However, at this time he brought in his first dream, which did help him to get in touch with some of his resentment toward me. In the dream one of Al's patients, a man who was very angry with Al, was physically beating himself up instead. Although in discussing the dream Al tried to focus his attention on his patient's negative transference, I was able to show Al that he was the patient in the dream, protecting me from his aggression and hurting himself instead.

Al, although accepting the interpretation that he was the masochistic patient in the dream, still remained quite inhibited in our sessions. I suggested that he was still somewhat afraid to show me his hostile fantasies, particularly those toward me. When he thought about my interpretation, Al believed that if he revealed his aggressive fantasies, he would beat me "to a pulp." He feared that he could overwhelm me with his sadism and frighten me so much that I would not be able to function as his therapist!

Al was clearly worried about doing to me what he himself had experienced many times—make me the vulnerable, weak child to be dominated by him—"a reversal of roles" (A. Freud, 1946). Because I believed it was important for Al to see that I was not too terrified of his sadism but wanted to understand it instead, I asked Al how he would feel about seeing me more often so that we could discuss his hostile fantasies more and understand them better. Al told me that he had been thinking about this possibility himself, and without any overt resistance he made arrangements to see me three times a week.

ON THE COUCH

With Al seeing me more often, I felt that he could now tolerate the regression induced by the couch, which would enable him to get to material that greatly influenced his life but was essentially unconscious. Similar to his positive response to the idea of increasing the frequency of the sessions, Al had no difficulty moving from sitting up and facing me to lying down and having me be unseen.

At first Al welcomed free associating on the couch and took pleasure in examining his dreams and fantasies. He reported that once again his relationships at home and work were going well and he was pleased with himself and the life he was leading. But by the time we were into the ninth month of treatment and Al had been using the couch for over a month, he began once again to question me and the analysis. Al felt I had "trapped" him, made him feel weak by "manipulating" him into "a passive position" on the couch. I was doing all of this to strengthen my "weak ego" at his expense.

The position of being on the couch made Al feel he was "a victimized slave." He berated me for making him feel that he was "back home again," being demeaned and belittled by his family. Furthermore, I was forcing him to work, and he wanted some leisure time. In a dream he had during his tenth month of treatment, Al made himself into a Black slave who was singing, "You and me, we sweat and toil, get a little drunk and land in jail." Al was not only a slave in his mind, but a prisoner who had to be wary of when I would inflict punishment on him.

As Al's masochistic modus vivendi was asserting itself much more in the treatment situation, I eventually was able to help him to question why he held onto it with so much tenacity. He thought that if he worked hard like a slave, he would be loved by parental figures and sibling substitutes. He recalled as a child often vowing to work harder so that he would be loved.

But Al resented the idea of having to work hard in order to be loved. He felt this resentment with me and with many others as well. "You know damn well you'd have nothing to do with me if I did not pay and give you the material you want to hear," bellowed Al in the thirteenth month of treatment. He went on to say, "But I hate you for making me work hard and accepting me so conditionally. That's why I hate this treatment and want to jump off the couch, tell you to go to hell, and never come back."

The intensity of the sadism ("the wolf") that was behind Al's masochism ("the lambskin") was quite powerful. For many weeks and months, Al brought out wishes to torture me, castrate me, kill me, and bury me. When I did not comment on his murderous wishes toward me, he began to experience them toward his parents, brothers, and then later toward his colleagues and supervisors. He felt that he had been everybody's "pawn" but he secretly wanted to be a "tyrannical king."

By the time Al had been in treatment 18 months, he had managed to fantasy maiming and eventually destroying virtually everybody he knew including, of course, his wife Sharon and his daughter Becky.

As Al discharged his sadistic fantasies, from time to time he found himself identifying with the most ruthless sadist in history, Adolph Hitler. In his identification with Hitler, Al wanted "to torture my Jewish parents, Jewish brothers, and all those who made me feel weak, deprived, and powerless."

The similarity of Al's dynamics to Hitler's was not just idle speculation on Al's part. In his book, *The Life and Death of Adolph Hitler,* Payne said about Hitler's character:

> If he resembled anyone at all, it was Dostoevsky's ill-tempered "underground man," the man who comes out from under the floor boards, who thirsts for power and is powerless, desires to torture and be tortured, to debase himself and to debase others, to be proud and to humble himself (Payne, 1973, p. 172).

As Al pondered the character of Hitler and embarrassingly confessed his kinship to him, he recognized Hitler's deep desire for love as well as his own. Al believed that if an individual feels loved, he or she would not become sadistic. Al could have added that if an individual does not love those toward whom he or she is sadistic, punishment would not have to follow in the form of masochistic behavior. This was blatantly observed in Hitler's sexual activities with his mistress; daily, he would enjoy being whipped by her (Saul, 1976).

THE YEARNING FOR LOVE

By the time Al had been in treatment with me for two years, he realized that what had been sorely missing from his life were love relationships. There had been a great deal of hatred in his home as a child and this seemed to be the situation in his current family life with Sharon and Becky. Hatred also seemed to be a major component in his relationships at work as well. Al constantly reiterated, "Being deprived [of love] made me depraved."

Not only did Al become aware of his hunger to love and be loved, but he now realized, and with much conviction, that his sadism, and the masochism he used to defend against it, was his way of responding to the unresponsiveness, insensitivity, and lovelessness that came from many people in his life — past and present.

In his third year of therapy, Al brought out many fantasies demonstrating how much he yearned to be held, carressed, fondled, and have genital sex with me. Hesitant and mildly ashamed at first, Al was able to face how much he wanted to be a little boy with me and turn me into either a loving father, mother, or big brother. At times he fantasied himself as a little girl and made me a mother who had no children other than Al — a fantasy he had nurtured all of his life, which was to be an only child.

What seemed to predominate in Al's fantasies for loving contact were pregenital yearnings. Often Al fantasied himself as a baby at the breast, enjoying the sucking and pleasurably imbibing good milk. From time to time in his dreams and fantasies he would also be an infant who would urinate or defecate at any time or place he felt like doing so. Although Al occasionally discussed desires to have anal intercourse with me, in which he would invariably be in the passive position, he had frequent fantasies in which he would be enveloped by my body and we would mutually enjoy a blissful symbiosis.

In discussing the preponderance of his pregenital wishes, Al reminisced about what he believed was a very crucial time in his life, namely, his first year. He had the intuitive feeling, later corroborated by his mother, that when he was born his parents and his three older brothers made him "the mascot" of the family and fussed over him a great deal. But when he was less than one year old, the family members agreed that they were indulging Al too much and abruptly stopped giving him attention and affection.

Al felt that the abrupt withdrawal of love that he experienced early in life had served as a paradigm for all subsequent love relationships. He would invariably anticipate withdrawal and abandonment from those who loved him. And, just as Al had experienced many and intense pregenital yearnings when he was emotionally abandoned as a one-year-old, he was often in the same emotional position as an adult. Realizing this, he was now able to face some of the dynamic issues in his sexual liaisons with former patients.

AL'S AFFAIRS WITH FORMER PATIENTS

As was true in the treatment of virtually all of the therapists that I worked with who had had sexual contact with patients, it took Al a great deal of time before he could feel safe enough with me to examine those conflicts that led to his acting out with patients.

When Al decided to investigate some of the motives that sparked his affairs with patients, he had to make a confession first. He confessed that he had been sexually involved with another former patient for a few months while he was in treatment with me, in addition to the three affairs with patients that had taken place prior to our work.

Particularly because Al was begining to discuss some issues that were painful and difficult for him to face, I wanted to help him feel as comfortable with me as was possible. Therefore, first I investigated with him what I was doing in our work that made it difficult for him to tell me about his most recent liaison.

Needless to say, if Al and I were unaware of what had been inhibiting him in our sessions, he would not be able to reveal very much about highly charged material. In response to my question concerning the dangers for him in sharing the details of his last sexual contact with a former patient, Al pointed out that he was certain I would have been "against" his affair and he did not want to hear my "censuring" remarks.

Inasmuch as he was making me a punitive superego that would admonish him severely, I decided not to challenge what Al ascribed to me, but to accept it and see what I could learn about his superego prohibitions as they were projected onto me. Therefore, I asked him, "What is it about your love affairs that I'm against?" Al responded, "Not only do you probably think what I'm doing is unethical and unprofessional, but also you believe it is harmful to the patients and is neurotic on my part." Although Al was correct in what he ascribed to me, it was also clear that a part of him had convictions about sex with patients that were similar to mine. But as far as Al was concerned, it was only I who had reservations about his having affairs with patients. Consequently, we had to stay with and examine what he believed was my position, not his.

I next asked Al, "When you refer to my punitive attitudes toward you, could you tell me what I consider 'unethical,' 'unprofessional,' 'harmful,' and 'neurotic'?" Al responded, "I know enough about psychotherapy to realize when a therapist seeks out a patient to have an affair with her, he's doing something for himself, not for the patient. It certainly doesn't help a patient learn how to separate and to gain autonomy when the therapist runs after her when treatment ends. And you know damn well that if I weren't neurotic, I'd be having sex with Sharon, not with my patients."

Al mentioned that for a number of years, sex with Sharon was infrequent—sometimes weeks would go by without any contact. "I've got to admit that one of the reasons I sought out these women patients was because I was extremely lonely and I knew they would be glad to be with me and that would help me," Al acknowledged.

As Al discussed his loneliness further, he tearfully recalled how during his childhood and adolescence, in fact throughout his entire life, he had strong wishes "to be mothered," but felt "this was impossible to get." He thought when he married Sharon she could "take care" of him, but he experienced her as consistently "cold, aloof, and rejecting." This was also the way he experienced the few young women he dated a few times prior to his marriage.

As Al described in detail the warm and loving responses he received from his former patients, which seemed like unusual but extremely valuable gifts to him, he became sensitized to the major countertransference themes that propelled his intense desires to have affairs with them. Al experienced these women patient-lovers as "loving and lovable mothers." "And what was terrific," said Al with pride and much excitement, "is I had them all to myself." Al also informed me that one of his dominant and persistent fantasies when having sex with his women patients was "grabbing" his mother and aggressively taking her away from his brothers and father. Often he proudly said to himself when with a woman patient in bed, "She is mine, not theirs."

When Al talked about "possessing" his women patients, he could face the sense of triumph he felt over his brothers and father and in this regard, referred to himself as "Al the Conqueror." As a conqueror who debased his father and brothers, Al recognized that he made his professional colleagues and supervisors "brothers and fathers who get under my skin" and "I'm really laughing at them, perhaps even gloating."

During the course of examining rivalrous feelings toward his brothers and father, Al brought in a dream that involved this theme. In the dream, which occurred toward the end of his third year of therapy, Al was in a taxicab as a passenger, hostilely giving directions to the driver. His associations to the dream led to wishes to yell at and demean his father who had been a taxicab driver in reality. Al talked about secretly feeling a continual condescending attitude toward his father most of his life but felt guilty and ashamed of his derogatory attitude "to that nice old guy."

I suggested to Al that the setting of a taxicab with one person in the back and another in the front was similar to the analytic situation with one person in front and the other "in the back seat." Al, intrigued with my suggestion, stated with some agitation, "I guess I've made you the patient and I'm the analyst. The father is the driver and the son is the slave-driver!"

Al and I frequently referred later to what we called "the taxicab dream." It was a condensation of Al's phallic oedipal wishes which he had kept far away from himself and others. All of the sadism that he had defended against by being depressed, servile, obsequious, and masochistic was embodied in that dream. By going over it frequently we could help Al face his sadism and feel less afraid of asserting himself.

A LOOK AT AL'S MARITAL CONFLICTS

It was not until Al was in his fourth year of treatment that he could face his marital conflicts with Sharon. Sharon was a librarian, whom Al described as kind, bright, and "non-libidinal." However, as Al could see how much investment he had in keeping her as an asexual mother, he became less provocative and less rejecting of her. When Sharon was demeaned less, she became more loving and more sexual. At first Al responded very positively to Sharon's warmth and increased interest in sex. But after a few weeks, Al retreated. At first, he rationalized his withdrawal by pointing out that Sharon was becoming cold again. Yet, his dreams clearly demonstrated that he was afraid of living with a sexual mother figure. In one dream he was moving away from a naked older woman and in another dream he kept calling Sharon "Mother."

Al had to face incestuous feelings toward his mother, and this was very difficult for him to do. He had a great deal of hostility toward his mother and in facing and acknowledging sexual and loving feelings toward her, he felt that this would be "giving her too much power." When I pointed out to Al that his mother,

Sharon, or any woman appeared too powerful only when he made himself a little boy, he began to face and slowly to give up some of his passive wishes to remain small and have "a big Mama."

When Al had faced many of his secret oedipal issues, his marriage improved a great deal and he felt more relaxed with Becky as well.

TERMINATION

Having given up the idea of having affairs with patients, seeing his marriage improve, observing his relationship with his daughter begin to blossom, and starting to have a successful private practice as well as an important administrative job at the Center, Al was ready to terminate treatment after four and a half years.

Termination was a very difficult process for Al and took over seven months. Al vacillated between two extreme positions. Either he wanted to leave treatment without any discussion whatsoever of termination or else he wanted to stay in treatment forever.

As we analyzed Al's two very contradictory attitudes, it eventually became clear that the reason he was adamant about terminating quickly was to avoid confronting his deep attachment to me and his strong wish to remain my child forever. "If I allow myself to see how much I love you and want you," Al lamented, "then termination of treatment will be too traumatic for me."

During the termination phase, Al brought out many fantasies of clinging to me, sucking my fantasied breasts, sitting on my lap, and being anally penetrated by my penis and fingers. When I remained quite silent as he freely associated to being my baby, young boy, and young girl, he eventually saw that he was "chasing a rainbow." After five years of therapy, Al ended treatment with his life very different from when he began it.

ASSESSMENT OF AL'S THERAPY

In terms of Al's functioning as measured by the components of the analytic ideal (Fine, 1982), Al was able to love much more maturely by the end of his therapy. His sadomasochistic modus vivendi had diminished considerably in all of his work and family relationships. He could have realistic pleasure and did not need to abuse his patients or feel abused by Sharon, his colleagues, or his supervisors. His consistently depressed affect paled, and he began to show a wide range of emotions. People now were communicating well with him and he with them. He was particularly relating well sexually and interpersonally with Sharon. Symptoms had disappeared and he had become a solid man playing an active role in his family, at work, and in the community.

CHAPTER **VI**

CONCLUSIONS
Treatment Principles,
Cautionary Notes, and
Preventive Measures

As we embark on the last leg of our journey, it may be beneficial for us, the travelers, to review briefly why we decided to take this voyage and to restate what we hoped to gain from it.

Our major reason for initiating this project was our concern that the therapist who acts out sexually with his or her patients has been treated by colleagues and superiors all too frequently in a punitive, nontherapeutic manner. Though not wishing to ignore or condone the profoundly negative impact on the patient who is exploited sexually by the clinician, the major focus of the study was on the dynamics and treatment of the therapist who engages in sexual activity with patients.

Coping with sexual impulses and sexual fantasies toward patients has been a perennial problem of mental health professionals ever since the inception of psychotherapy. Until most recently, the subject has been virtually ignored, and, as a result, the fantasies, anxieties, defenses, conflicts, history, training, and personal therapy of clinicians who act out sexually with their patients have been shrouded in secrecy. In this project, it was our wish to unearth this material and relate to it with empathy and objectivity.

Because sexually acting-out therapists have not been com-passionately studied on a case-by-case basis, the way many

154

other patient populations of mental health professionals have been, their numbers have not decreased and the problems they pose to their clientele, to their colleagues, to their professional organizations, and to themselves tend to persist.

In preparing for our journey we learned that sexual acting out with patients was very popular among the professionals of Freud's inner circle. Rank, Jung, Jones, Ferenczi, as well as others from his group, had sexual contacts with their patients (Grosskurth, 1991). What is noteworthy about this past "state of affairs" is that this has been more than replicated by the followers of Freud's inner circle and by current psychotherapists as well. At least 10% to 20% of those clinicians who have been queried on the subject acknowledge sexual activity with their patients (Gabbard, 1989). Furthermore, their numbers are probably higher, inasmuch as many psychotherapists, despite being granted anonymity, are frightened to tell the truth for fear of retribution (Gabbard, 1989; Rutter, 1989).

In a study by Pope and Vetter (1991) entitled "Prior Therapist-Patient Sexual Involvement Among Patients Seen by Psychologists," the authors discovered that approximately half of the 647 psychologists they interviewed, all of whom where involved in clinical or counseling services, recalled treating at least one patient who had been sexually intimate with a prior therapist. Respondents also pointed out that 90% of the 1,000 cases involving sexual intimacy between therapist and patient that they discussed with the investigators proved harmful to the patient. Only 12% of the patients who had been sexually involved with a prior therapist and received treatment filed formal ethics or legal complaints.

Although we are not aware of the full extent of patient-therapist sexual contact, we have become increasingly sensitive to the emotional scars that are inflicted on the patient. Often the victim, usually a woman, appears similar to a battered child who has been emotionally abused and sexually exploited by a parental figure (Bates & Brodsky, 1989; Freeman & Roy, 1976; Rutter, 1989).

A dramatic shift in attitude toward therapists who have sex

with their patients is widespread among the current therapeutic community. In contrast to the laissez-faire attitude that was shown toward clinicians such as Jung, Rank and other members of Freud's inner circle, today's sexually acting-out psychotherapists are subject to lawsuits, loss of their licenses, disbarment from professional organizations, and other retaliatory measures.

As we travelled further on our journey, we found several reasons to account for the shift in attitude toward the clinician who sexually exploits his or her patients. One of the most influential factors has been the feminist movement (Chesler, 1972). Sparked by the leadership of NOW and other social activists, women have been consistently speaking out against sexual harassment and sexual exploitation in industry, the military, education, politics, and in the family. Recognizing that they should not be compelled to submit to a subordinate, demeaned role at the workplace or elsewhere has helped women to be more assertive and self-confident as patients in psychotherapy and to feel entitled to question and to challenge "therapeutic harassment."

One of the by-products of our study is that we became increasingly aware of how effective women have been in the last two decades in securing the recognition and status they deserve and have earned. As one example, 1992 was often described as "The Year of the Woman in Politics," inasmuch as more women ran for elective office in the United States than ever before. This occurrence was in sharp contrast to the 1920s when dynamic psychotherapy was introduced to the United States and when women were feeling fortunate because they were "granted the right to vote."

Another example of how much progress has been made in enhancing women's rights is the increasing attention women are receiving in the media. In 1992 the three best-selling non-fiction books were *The Silent Passage* by Gail Sheehy (1992), which deals with the psychological and social significance of menopause for today's women; Gloria Steinem's (1992) *Revolution from Within*, a feminist's reflections on the struggle to achieve self-esteem; and *Backlash* by Susan Faludi (1992), who demonstrates that the media and political groups have been staging a war against women's rights.

As the revolt against sexism has become a powerful phenomenon in our society during the last couple of decades, concern has been expressed about the possibility of a latent sexism in the practice of psychotherapy (Karasu, 1980). The alleged sexism in psychotherapy may be reflected in the finding that the vast majority of professionals who have been reported to have had sex with their patients (96%) are male therapists exploiting female patients (Gabbard, 1989; Rutter, 1989). Concomitant with the recognition of sexism in psychotherapy has been the realization "that Freud's estimates of women's morality and objectivity are logically and empirically indefensible" (Schafer, 1992, p. 68).

In response to the changes in the broader culture that have helped to focus more attention on sex between therapists and patients, there have been several new developments in the mental health professions that make sex between clinician and patient a more salient topic. Practitioners now tend to view psychotherapeutic interaction as involving two vulnerable human beings who form a partnership. Therefore, not only do the patient's transference reactions influence the process and outcome of the therapy, but the practitioner's subjective countertransference reactions make a major contribution as well (Brenner, 1985; Schafer, 1992; Slakter, 1987; Teitelbaum, 1990).

As the therapeutic situation has been more carefully researched, the man or woman who becomes a psychotherapist has been investigated much more. What attracts individuals to the practice of psychotherapy has been explored in breadth and depth during the past two decades. It is well documented that many, if not most, psychotherapists have serious neurotic and interpersonal problems and in many cases suffer as much as or more than their patients (Bermak, 1977; Burton, 1972; Deutsch, 1984; Fine, 1982; Finell, 1985; Freudenberger & Robbins, 1979; Maeder, 1989; Searles, 1975; Strean, 1990). Thus it is now well recognized that the therapist can also resist the therapeutic process in ways similar to the patient and demonstrate many unresolved problems as well, such as the propensity to act out sexually.

In addition to the greater attention given to the therapeutic situation and the psychodynamics of the clinician, more consideration has been given to the limitations and problems inherent in psychoanalytic and psychotherapeutic training programs, some of which may contribute to the sexual acting out of therapists with patients. Our review of the literature demonstrates that as psychotherapists in training constantly experience their own mentors crossing the boundaries of disciplined therapeutic interaction, they are more prone to participate in violating the norms that govern the conduct of sound clinical work.

In the existing literature on the issue before us, we witnessed two opposing trends in the psychotherapeutic field during the last two decades. In the 1970s many therapists were advocating hugging, kissing, and other forms of bodily contact as a means of resolving their patients' resistances, increasing their self-esteem, enhancing their sexual performance, and improving their interpersonal relationships (Masters & Johnson, 1970; Mintz, 1969; Shepard, 1971). By the 1980s, however, these practices met with strong opposition in many circles. The sensitivity and encounter movements were questioned (Kovel, 1976) and writers like Shepard (1971) were reprimanded and repudiated (Bates & Brodsky, 1989). Many authors began to point out that the erotic transference was often "a bid for re-assurance, a cover-up for hostility, an expression of penis envy, an oral-incorporative wish, a defense against homosexuality and all of these at different times" (Fine, 1982, p. 95). They also suggested that the many patients who talked about sex a great deal and made many sexual demands on the therapist were often sexually starved (Karasu & Socarides, 1979). Of course, these statements and explanations concerning the patient's sexual problems could be and were applied to the therapist and to his or her erotic countertransference.

With psychotherapy coming under a great deal of public scrutiny during the past two decades, patients have been more outspoken about their psychological and legal rights as consumers of psychotherapy (Freeman & Roy, 1976; Plasil, 1985). As a result, more information has been gathered on the psychotherapist who sexually exploits his or her patients. The modal therapist involved sexually with patients is a middle-aged man who is typically about 15 years older than the patient. Usually this clinician is very unhappy with his own love relationships, has a poor marriage, and/or may be going through a divorce proceeding. Although he has experienced a great deal of conflict in his interpersonal relationships with women, his practice is predominated by women patients, and he is likely to be involved sexually with more than one patient at a time (Brodsky, 1989; Gabbard, 1989; Sussman, 1992).

The sexually exploitative therapist also tends to be a professional who behaves in many antitherapeutic ways. He arranges for patients to advise him on financial matters, work for him, and he may even socialize with patients (Brodsky, 1989). He also tends to disclose features of his interpersonal life to his patients, particularly areas such as his marital conflict (Twemlow & Gabbard, 1989). Despite his readiness to discuss his personal and interpersonal problems with patients, the sexualizing practitioner tends to be an isolated professional (Brodsky, 1989). Even if he works in a clinic or an agency, he does not consult too much with his peers—perhaps because he is extremely preoccupied with being discovered. Although he does not emerge as a very sensitive or competent sexual partner (Bates & Brodsky, 1989; Fine, 1982; Freeman & Roy, 1976; Plasil, 1985), the sexually acting-out clinician is idealized and loved for long periods of time by the women patients with whom he has affairs.

As was pointed out earlier in this chapter, the main objective of this project was to secure more detailed information about the psychodynamics and treatment of the therapist who sexually exploits his or her patients. With this objective in mind, four representative cases were selected (from over 75 that have come to my attention professionally).

For several reasons, the cases of Ron, Roslyn, Bob, and Al may be viewed as a skewed sample. First, with the exception of Al, all of them were individuals who sought personal therapy rather than having been mandated to secure it. We know now that it is the healthier, more mature individual who has the strength to ask for therapeutic help and the courage to face himself or herself (Fine, 1982; Kadushin, 1969; Strean, 1980). Consequently, whatever inferences can be derived from the sample may be applied only to those psychotherapists who have the inner freedom and ego strengths to confront themselves in treatment. Second, the sample, as suggested, is very small, comes from one city, New York, and was treated by one person. Therefore, my own prejudices, idiosyncrasies, and countertransference reactions color the findings. Third, the theoretical perspective that governs my professional work is classically Freudian. Whatever biases and limitations that are inherent in this orientation, of which I am not completely aware, have affected my interpretations of the data, as well as my therapeutic interventions with the therapists under examination.

With some of the above limitations of this project now borne in mind, what can we say about the therapists presented? I believe this sample, though skewed, has taught us a great deal about the psychodynamics of the sexually exploitative clinician and how he or she may be helped to resolve the conflicts that have contributed to his or her self-destructive and sexually abusive behavior. In this chapter, as the title suggests, in addition to a review of my patients' dynamics, I would like to present some principles that I have learned from the cases under study, and suggest some cautions to keep in mind when treating therapists who have had sex with their patients.

One of the most obvious features of all of our "therapist-patients" was that each of them had serious problems in loving. None of them could sustain mature, loving relationships with his or her spouse, or consistently love children, colleagues, friends, or relatives. All of the subjects had very disturbed sexual lives, harbored a great deal of hatred toward many individuals in their past and/or present milieus, and in many ways were childishly narcissistic people who could not relate to their patients with sustained empathy, objectivity, or appropriate restraint.

All four of the clinicians studied showed a great deal of self-hate. Although it varied in frequency and intensity, depression emerged in all of them. Sadomasochism was a common theme in the interpersonal relationships of the subjects and was extremely strong in one case, Al.

When we examine several dimensions of their past and present functioning, our "therapist-patients" emerge with much in common. Let us now review some of their common characteristics.

PSYCHOSEXUAL DEVELOPMENT

One of the impressive findings of our study is that all of the subjects had very ungratifying relationships with both of their parents. Their mothers appeared to be egocentric, unempathetic, and unable to provide the consistent, tender love and care that toddlers absolutely need. The fathers of our subjects could be characterized as either detached and passive and/or excessively punitive. As a result, our subjects became adults who were starved for love, particularly for bodily contact. They were swamped by the demands of their primitive wishes that clamored constantly for gratification. All of our subjects were in a rage because their strong wishes for emotional and bodily contact were not being gratified. During the course of their therapy, they showed what Erikson (1950) called "a lack of inner certainty" and "a basic mistrust" of people.

Prominent writers such as Melanie Klein (1957) and Margaret Mahler (1968) pointed out that when there is insufficient and inconsistent gratification from parents during the early years, depression is a very common result. It is something we observed in all of our subjects. Further, as Harlow (1974) convincingly demonstrated, when early bodily experiences are frustrating and painful, they have a decisive effect on later genital experience. This seems to have occurred with Al particularly, definitely with Bob, and to some extent with Roslyn and Ron. Interestingly, the latter two therapists, although pained by early deprivation, tended to receive a little more gratification from their parents than Al and Bob did and seemed to function a little better in their interpersonal relationships with both patients and nonpatients.

As we worked with our "therapist-patients," they all appeared to have suffered from strong feelings of loneliness—a loneliness that existed from early childhood to the time they came for additional therapy with me. This loneliness, they felt as adults, could be penetrated by nothing except the sexual ecstasy of the highest intensity. The desperation and emptiness in their lives were so great that they were ready to sacrifice an enormous amount in order to receive the joy they craved (Griffin, 1992).

It is well known among psychodynamically oriented clinicians and others that when a youngster has been generously given to emotionally and physically during the early stages of life, he or she more easily becomes a cooperative, caring individual. Our subjects who were thwarted in their early stages of life, as well as during later stages, became quite antagonistic toward others, sometimes overtly and at other times covertly. All of them tended to show more than the average amount of obstinacy, defiance, rebelliousness, self-will, and hostility to authority (Fine, 1975).

A marked characteristic that our subjects held in common was bisexuality—the result of problems with sexual identity. This is not surprising because if a child is to enjoy his or her sexual identity, the youngster needs generous amounts of reinforcement or "mirroring" from parents (Kohut, 1977). All of our subjects, as already mentioned, did not feel well accepted by either parent. When the men therapists, as boys, moved toward their mothers and wanted to be considered as lovable and sexual young men, their mothers' hatred, anxiety, and narcissism prevented them from responding in a relaxed, mature manner. As a result these boys regressed toward homosexual preoccupations. Inasmuch as their homosexual fantasies created intense anxiety for them, they needed to ward off all kinds of inner doubts by appearing very "masculine." The same sort of problems existed with our female therapist, Roslyn. Her father was not emotionally responsive to her and "helped" her regress to homosexual preoccupations. These preoccupations induced many anxieties, which forced her to construct different types of maladaptive defenses.

Love that can be characterized as mature takes place when the individual has conscious control over his or her feelings. The mature man or woman is not carried away by love; he or she loves. Reuben Fine (1975) suggests that love goes through five stages of development: attachment, admiration, mutual enjoyment, intimacy, and devotion. These five ingredients enter into the adult feeling of love and they can be mixed in varying measures; these mixtures determine the sincerity and adequacy of any love relationship.

Applying Fine's perspective on the stages of love to our subjects, we can better understand their defective psychosexual development. Unable in their earlier years to experience warm attachments, particularly to their mothers, they responded to this deprivation with much hatred and mistrust toward others. Because of an inadequate pregenital base, they could not form a loving evaluation of their parents, that is, they could not admire them. As Fine states:

> In a loving family, the normal result of the oedipal period is penis pride rather than castration anxiety, vaginal pleasure rather than penis envy. This phase lasts all through the latency period, and in greater or lesser degree is incorporated into all love relationships later on in life. (1975, p. 18).

When the stages of attachment and admiration are essentially gratifying, the boy or girl at puberty is able to begin enjoying the opposite sex. Our subjects were never able to enjoy the opposite sex freely and spontaneously from puberty to their middle adult years. For them, sexuality provoked anxiety, self-doubt, and vulnerability. It blocked the smooth exchange with the opposite sex of feelings, hopes, attitudes, and dreams, all of which are part of an intimate relationship.

Devotion, which necessitates a greater concern for the welfare of the other person than for one's self, was very weak in all of our subjects. As angry, hypersensitive, and egocentric people, they could not be devoted spouses, parents, friends, or therapists.

MARITAL RELATIONSHIPS

Most clinicians agree that only happy people can have happy marriages. Our subjects, all of whom were unhappy individuals, had hateful relationships with their mates. They had many chronic complaints toward them and failed to see that what they resented about their mates they helped to arrange, albeit unconsciously. For example, Ron constantly complained about his wife's asexuality, but he "needed" her to be this way in order to ward off his own incestuous feelings and castration anxiety. Roslyn, who debased her husband generally, "needed" to see him as weak in order to foster her own competition with men.

With the exception of Al, all of our "therapist-patients" had extramarital relationships prior to becoming involved sexually with their patients. In so doing, they were expressing not only their ambivalence toward their marital partners, but also they were revealing their inability to separate emotionally from them and to feel autonomous. In their marriages, our subjects were reminiscent of the marital dyad in Albee's play, *Who Is Afraid of Virginia Woolf?* This couple fought with each other for 20 years, had a very poor sexual relationship, were involved in extramarital affairs, but they could not tolerate any form of separation from each other. They were too childish to feel or to be autonomous and argued with each other for hours at a time.

In many ways our subjects unconsciously turned their marital partners into hated parental figures. Feeling like victimized children, they sought solace in their extramarital affairs and later in affairs with patients. Their extramarital partners and patients were experienced as psychological children like themselves and did not threaten them as much as their marital partners, who were perceived as overbearing and overwhelming parental figures.

OTHER INTERPERSONAL RELATIONSHIPS

Another glaring characteristic of the men and woman we studied is that none of them had close, warm, spontaneous relationships with virtually anybody. With their hatred strong and their childish yearnings great, they found it difficult to feel close to their children, colleagues, family, or neighbors. Rarely did any of them speak of close friends. Thus, one of the important findings of our study is that the subjects had weak object relationships. Unable to internalize warm objects into their psychic structures, our "therapist-patients" often appeared in their therapy as individuals without deep emotional ties to anyone. They hated their parents, felt distant from their siblings, and as children and later as adults were close to friendless. Their experiences with the therapists they chose to treat them, like their other relationships, were essentially unsuccessful. In sum, our sample could be described as consisting of individuals without much of "an object world" (Jacobson, 1964).

A little later in this chapter, we will provide a detailed dynamic explanation to account for our subjects' sexual exploitation of their patients. In this section, we wish to focus on their more general attitudes toward work and on some of their professional behavior.

With the possible exception of Al, our subjects could be considered in many ways as competent mental health practitioners. They all had graduate degrees and all had participated in postgraduate in-service training. Two of the four had extensive and intensive psychoanalytic training.

Although our subjects were social isolates in their work, as other writers have found sexually exploitative therapists to be

(Brodsky, 1989; Gabbard, 1989), all of them nonetheless were interested in the professional literature, attended professional conferences, and tried to secure suitable supervision to enhance their clinical skills. Unlike sexually acting-out therapists reported by other researchers (Brodsky, 1989; Sussman, 1992), not all of our subjects were antitherapeutic with all of their patients. They selected one or two patients to disclose information about themselves and were excessively gratifying with some, not with all of their patients. Of the four subjects, only Bob reported having sex with more than two patients, although Al did have sexual contact with three patients after their treatment terminated.

It was my strong impression that although our subjects were not excessively gratifying with all of their patients, they were overactive therapists. They talked too much, intervened more than was necessary, and gave advice and counsel too frequently. None of them consistently showed the necessary frustration tolerance and appropriate impulse control that are regarded as essential requirements for the performance of sound therapy. All of our subjects seemed to become quite anxious when their patients revealed id material. Consequently, to diminish their discomfort, they intervened too often in sessions, finding therapeutic abstinence a difficult task with which to cope.

EGO AND SUPEREGO FUNCTIONS

All four of our subjects had fragmented egos. Some of their ego functions worked well some of the time, while the same and other ego functions did not work well at other times. For example, in their work with most of their patients much of the time, our subjects used good judgment, had a good grasp of reality, adapted to the requirements of the clinical situation, and used defenses that were adaptive. However, as we have noted repeatedly, when they indulged, overgratified, or had sexual contact with their patients, their judgment at these times was impaired, they could not realistically differentiate a patient from a lover, and they regressed enormously.

Some of the most obvious impairments in the ego functioning of our therapist-patients were their poor impulse control and their weak frustration tolerance. This not only became apparent in their sexual acting out with patients but in their inability to monitor their wishes to intervene frequently in the therapy. They were poor listeners and appeared close to being compulsive talkers.

The same fragmented ego functioning noted in their work was also apparent in our subjects' marriages. They distorted their mates and related to them as if they were omnipotent parents. Acting as children in their marriages, our subjects became easily angered with their mates, showed limited monitoring of infantile wishes and continually collected injustices, emerging fairly frequently as quite paranoid.

As we have already suggested, our subjects' weakest ego function was in the area of object relations. Their infantile narcissism pervaded much of their activity in work and love relationships, so that it was difficult for them to relate to anyone in a mature manner on a sustained basis.

Although some authors suggest that the sexually acting-out therapist is at times psychopathic (Brodsky, 1989; Gabbard, 1989), implying they are suffering from superego lacunae, this was not our finding. On the contrary, our therapist-patients seemed to have very punitive superegos that inhibited their pleasure and dampened their spontaneity in most interpersonal situations. In many ways, their rebellious behavior was a way of trying to challenge and attack the punitive voices of their active superegos.

All of our subjects suffered from low self-esteem and weak body images. Again, their overactive and rebellious behavior seemed to be an attempt to compensate for their feelings of low self-worth and pervasive guilt. Regarding their pervasive guilt, it is important to reiterate that none of them happily and freely had sex with their patients. All of them were conflicted and suffered from remorse, even though the remorse was not always apparent.

A DYNAMIC EXPLANATION OF THE
SEXUALLY EXPLOITATIVE THERAPIST

Despite the fact that no two individuals are the same dynamically, there appear to be many commonalities in the psychodynamics of our therapist-patients that may account for their sexually acting out behavior with patients.

The most obvious characteristic of all of our subjects is that they were starved for love. Unable to receive it from their spouses who appeared to them as punitive and overbearing parents, emotionally distant from their friends, colleagues, and family, they turned to their patients for emotional and sexual gratification. What was it about their patients that drove them to sexually act out with them?

One of the unique features of a psychotherapeutic relationship, regardless of the practitioner's theoretical perspective, is that many, if not most, patients tend to idealize the therapist to an enormous degree. Because the therapist listens empathically in a nonjudgmental manner, he or she often emerges as the perfect parent whom the patient has been desperately seeking, usually for a lifetime. To the therapist with low self-esteem and a weak body image, who in addition is extremely lonely, the patient's intense love and admiration, which the therapist has never come close to receiving heretofore, is like delicious food and drink to a starving and thirsty man or woman on a barren desert.

Not only is the therapist-patient under examination extremely grateful for the love, admiration, and idealization—all of which have been experienced as precious gifts from the patient—but the love that the therapist-patient feels toward the patient is also unique. The therapist strongly identifies with the love-starved patient with whom he or she has much in common. Consequently, there is frequently a strong narcissistic attraction between two individuals who are very vulnerable, weak, and lonely and who seem to need each other for very similar reasons.

Ron, Roslyn, Bob, and Al all pointed out in their therapy with me that they found themselves loving their patients the way they wished to be loved either by their parents, spouses, or their own therapists. The manna from heaven they thought they were providing their patients was the manna they desperately wanted for themselves. They were like hungry parents over-indulging their children with harmful food.

The strong narcissistic identification that the sexually acting-out therapist has with the patient may explain the infatuation with the therapeutic partner, but it does not fully account for the sexual involvement with the patient. The sexual involvement that emanates from a mutual infatuation, I believe, is an overdetermined phenomenon.

As stated previously, the sexually acting-out therapist has been frustrated and deprived during early childhood. Consequently, he or she craves for bodily satisfaction that seems to have been missing during an entire lifetime. However, the therapist-patient cannot feel comfortable receiving bodily satisfaction from an adult like his or her spouse because the latter is so often experienced as a punitive and overbearing parent. Inasmuch as all of our subjects felt like deprived children with depriving adults in most interpersonal situations, their patients, who appeared like children to them, seemed to be the least threatening sexual partners they could find. In this respect, the sexually acting-out therapist is very similar to a child molester or sexually abusing parent (Bates & Brodsky, 1989; Gabbard, 1989; Sussman, 1992), who experiences children as much less intimidating sexual partners than adults.

The therapist who has sexual liaisons with patients is an individual who suffers a great deal from an unstable sexual identity: the male patient-therapist has strong unconscious fantasies to be a sexual woman, and the female patient-therapist has strong unconscious fantasies to be a sexual man. It is enormously reassuring to those therapists who have many doubts about their sexual identities to have an attractive member of the opposite sex fall in love with them and have an intense erotic transference toward them. For a male therapist to be told he is the sexiest, most lovable man on earth is an enormous boon to his self-esteem. And when the admiring patient appears so soothing and engaging, it is very tempting to act out one's erotic desires with her. The woman therapist who has bisexual difficulties also welcomes the reassurance and seeming validation of an appealing male patient.

What is frequently overlooked in the sexual acting out between therapist and patient is that the male therapist, by having sex with a female patient, is gratifying, through identification, "the female in himself." The female therapist is also doing something similar with her male patient. Furthermore, patients who idealize their therapists and have sex with them unconsciously gratify "the therapist in themselves." For example, the woman patient who has sex with her male therapist unconsciously gratifies "the male therapist in herself" and feels ecstatic identifying with the superhuman image that she has ascribed to the therapist. The therapist, although not really understanding that the patient's ecstacy emanates from her irrational projections, nonetheless feels like a perfect lover and great man. This process is what Kohut (1977) refers to as "projective identification" in both parties whereby they attempt to have their "selves restored."

Another factor that motivates the therapist to act out sexually with the patient is his or her hostility toward the opposite sex. Ron, Roslyn, Bob, and Al all had considerable hatred toward the opposite sex. By exploiting their patients instead of helping them therapeutically, and gratifying themselves instead of fulfilling their professional assignments, they were in effect saying, "I will not help you; I will help myself. If that hurts you, it's too bad!"

We have alluded several times in this study to the hostility that the sexually acting-out clinician feels toward his or her profession and the practice of psychotherapy. Ron, Roslyn, Bob, and Al, at various times throughout our contacts, showed a strong contempt toward disciplined psychotherapy, frequently debased their supervisors and teachers, and often questioned traditional procedures to which most psychotherapists of any theoretical bent adhere.

In addition to harboring a great deal of animosity toward their patients and toward their profession, all of our subjects acted out considerable hostility toward their own previous therapists. In their rage toward their therapists, which often sounded quite similar to the rage they felt toward their parents, they seemed to be saying, "I wanted you to love me deeply and you did not! I hate you for depriving me of so much that is necessary! I'll show you what a good therapist (or parent) does! The good therapist, which I am and you are not, loves the patient (son or daughter) fully, unconditionally, with no holds barred!"

Although many therapists can become smitten with their patients and entertain intense sexual fantasies toward them, why did the clinicians in our study act out their erotic counter-transference wishes rather than try to analyze them, master them, and use them to benefit their patients? It should be remembered that all of our subjects had been doing therapy for many years before they became sexually involved with certain patients. I believe that as they entered the middle years of adulthood and felt many of their strengths waning and hopes being dashed, their lifelong rage, depression, feelings of loss and loneliness became most acute. After our therapist-patients tried extramarital affairs without deriving too much pleasure (in three out of four of the cases), their sexual acting out with patients may be viewed as an extreme act of desperation to fill a lifelong vacuum of an essentially loveless life.

As most psychotherapists recognize, acting out usually emerges when the patient cannot put into words what he or she feels and thinks. By the time our therapist-patients acted out with patients, they had progressively regressed to a preverbal stage of development. For our subjects, this preverbal stage can be described as one where they were acutely frustrated and craved soothing physical comfort and other forms of bodily attention and stimulation, but they had received only limited doses of it. Our subjects, just as they could not talk about their feelings and wishes when they were preverbal toddlers, could not with freedom and trust talk over with anyone what they emotionally experienced with their patients—specifically what they wanted to do with them sexually and emotionally.

As you may recall, one of Freud's earlier contributions (1914) was his explanation of the phenomenon of acting out. He suggested that patients who act out cannot cope with the pain and other emotions that verbalizing what is on their minds entails. Freud thought the conflicts that the acting-out patient dreads discussing "originated in the preverbal period" (1914, p. 146).

A motive that all of our subjects shared in their sexual acting out with patients is revenge. Here, we are in agreement with Hull and his colleagues who point out in a paper we referred to earlier, "Sexual Acting Out and the Desire for Revenge" (Hull, Lane, & Okie, 1989), that the primary motive in sexually acting out "is to get revenge against the analyst and other objects for present and past disappointments" (p. 317).

In addition to the destructive motive, sexual acting out can help a depressed person feel more alive (Coen, 1981). The specialness of the sexual relationship seems to obscure the individual's deficiencies in relating to others. This was noteworthy in all of our subjects.

Kaplan (1991), in a paper "Greed: A Psychoanalytic Perspective," describes greed as relating "to a process of acquiring or wanting possessions with an almost wanton disregard for the feelings of others" (p. 505). Though he demonstrates that greed may emerge from unresolved conflicts at all levels of psychosexual development, Kaplan implies that the greedy person is essentially an oral baby who feels very deprived but very entitled. These feelings of deprivation and entitlement were also observed consistently in our therapist-patients.

Melanie Klein's (1957) view of greed also seems applicable to our sample of therapist-patients. Klein saw greed as an "insatiable craving" that exceeds what a person needs and, in addition, exceeds what the object is usually willing to give. Its aim is to extract all of the goodness that can be taken from the object, who is rarely recognized as a person with unique rights of his or her own.

One of the findings of this study that tends to be corroborated by other researchers is that very few therapist-patient dyads who have sexual affairs continue their romances indefinitely. This suggests that therapists who act out sexually with their patients are not primarily interested in a sustained love relationship but seem to be more intent in having sex and then abandoning the patient. This illustrates a defense our subjects held in common, namely identification with the aggressor (A. Freud, 1946). Our subjects treated their patients in many ways the way they were sadistically treated by others (Fine, 1984).

Rutter (1989) in *Sex in the Forbidden Zone* points out that his research findings "suggest that the odds against a healthy marriage evolving from forbidden zone origins are almost insurmountable" (p. 175). He found that most of the liaisons he investigated lasted no more than six months. Although in our study we learned that the affair between therapist and patient can in some instances last longer, as a permanent love relationship it is usually bound to fail. Both parties are too childishly narcissistic to relate maturely to each other. Each does not see the partner realistically but tends to project infantile fantasies onto the other. These fantasies usually have very limited chance of being gratified in reality. The two individuals almost always have a great deal of unresolved hostility, revenge, depression, and desperation which seriously interfere with the possibility of having a rewarding, compassionate, and mature love relationship. Both require prolonged psychotherapy without any sexual contact, with a full and comprehensive exploration of their sexual fantasies and many sexual conflicts.

THE REHABILITATION AND TREATMENT OF THE SEXUALLY EXPLOITATIVE THERAPIST

The ethical and legal codes of all of the major mental health professions clearly state that sexual relationships between practitioners and patients are morally, ethically, and legally wrong. No responsible mental health professional in the 1990s can offer any legitimate rationale to justify sexual contact between therapist and patient. It helps neither. It harms both.

Sex between psychotherapist and patient as viewed by mental health professionals has had an interesting evolution. For many decades, when sexual contact between practitioner and patient was only occasionally exposed, most mental health professionals took the position that the patient, usually a female, was experiencing bizarre fantasies and her claims about being sexually exploited had limited and possibly no basis in reality. Furthermore, the therapist, even if it was shown that the patient had been sexually exploited, was usually exempt from legal or ethical charges.

By the 1970s numerous factors coalesced to change the view of mental health professionals toward sex between therapist and patient. Organizations that championed women's rights, social activists, and psychotherapy researchers, to name just a few groups interested in sexual harrassment and sexual abuse in its various forms, produced considerable and irrefutable evidence that sex between patient and therapist was indeed frequently a reality and had extremely deleterious effects on the victim (Freeman & Roy, 1976; Gabbard, 1989; Rutter, 1989; Sussman, 1992).

When child abuse and sexual abuse were acknowledged to be realities, it took some time before the dynamics and treatment of the abuser were considered. He or she was so abhorred and deplored that it was difficult to experience him or her as a frail and vulnerable human being who needed therapeutic attention. The child abuser or sex abuser understandably activated so much animosity in us that we sometimes forgot that if we were going to diminish the problem of abuse we needed to take a closer look at the perpetrator.

As psychotherapists we cannot be satisfied to limit our response to sexual exploitation of patients by saying it is wrong, harmful, deleterious to both parties, and deserving of ethical and legal sanctions. As with the child abuser and sex abuser, we need to understand the sexually exploitative therapist better and become clearer about how to rehabilitate him or her. In attempting to rehabilitate the emotionally disturbed practitioner who sexually abuses patients, we would be well advised to heed the admonitions of Kenneth Pope (1989a). In "Rehabilitation of Therapists Who Have Been Sexually Intimate with a Patient," Pope points out that legal and ethical procedures utilized against the perpetrator must be kept separate from his or her psychotherapy. As clinicians know, if the practitioner treats somebody who has violated legal or ethical codes but also participates in the individual's punishment, treatment will not and cannot be successful. It is sometimes overlooked that those who have committed crimes or participated in antisocial acts tend to view the therapist as a punitive superego. If therapists are also law enforcers, their therapeutic work will be resisted inasmuch as they will be realistically perceived, in part, as police officers.

As was seen in my treatment of Ron, Roslyn, Bob, and Al, they all viewed me at various times as a punitive superego who was more interested in punishing and berating them than in treating them. If I were also participating in enforcing the code of a professional organization or the laws of a particular city or state, treatment, in my opinion, would not have had any positive impact on them. Whenever transference fantasies toward the therapist are reinforced by reality, patients can no longer feel completely safe to reveal the truth about themselves; they are too wary about retribution.

It is a virtual axiom of dynamic psychotherapy that for patients to share confidences with a therapist they must experience the clinician as nonjudgmental and neutral. Particularly with sexually abusing therapists who have been condemned and castigated by many, it is imperative that they feel the practitioner has only one form of investment in their treatment—to help them understand themselves as well as possible. This is why Pope's (1989a) suggestion that the administration of justice be clearly separated from the therapy of the sexually exploitative therapist appears to be a sound and convincing one.

THE TREATMENT OF THE SEXUALLY EXPLOITATIVE
THERAPIST IS OFTEN INVOLUNTARY

In contrast to Ron, Roslyn and Bob, who referred themselves to me for psychotherapy (Al was referred to me by his supervisor), many sexually exploitative therapists are required to have therapy by law enforcement agencies, courts, and professional ethics committees. When treatment is mandated, it is extremely difficult for the practitioner to conduct it because the patient usually feels some or all of the following: accused, embarrassed, exposed, overpowered, demeaned, and resentful. Consequently, in contrast to the therapist-patients discussed in this study, those who are involuntary candidates for treatment need time to discuss many other resistances and to voice their strong resentment about being forced into the role of patient (Strean, 1990).

We saw in the treatment of the subjects of this study that it took them a long time to trust me fully. Those therapist-patients who do not seek psychotherapy for themselves would need even more time and attention to talk about their strong and many doubts about the value of psychotherapy than the subjects of our study. In addition, the conviction of these involuntary patients that they do not need therapeutic help must remain unchallenged and seen as a face-saving defense mechanism that they need to keep for some time. Often, these highly resistant, involuntary patients can move toward forming a therapeutic alliance with us when we spend a great deal of time and energy listening to them tell us why therapy does not work for most people, accepting their notion that they have already tried psychotherapy and it did not help them, and not challenging the idea that they received therapy in the past and now all of their problems have completely vanished!

A favorite resistance of involuntary therapist-patients is to question the skills and qualifications of those who are assigned to treat them. It is important to keep in mind that the patients before us are having their own skills and qualifications questioned by everyone around them. Therefore, rather than face the anxiety, humiliation, and punctured narcissism that this generates in them, sexually abusive therapists who become our patients prefer to displace and project their problems onto us. They would like to believe it is we who do not know how to do treatment, not they.

When our patients question our qualifications and skills, we should try to avoid becoming defensive and also attempt not to respond to their queries directly. Instead, we can tell these therapist-patients that as they know from their own clinical work, when skills and qualifications of the practitioner are questioned, the prospective patient has doubts about the therapist. Having said this, we can then ask, "What are your doubts about me?"

As is true with most individuals in therapy, when sexually exploitative therapists become patients, they are much more willing to involve themselves in treatment if their doubts about treatment are accepted as something they have a right to have and if their questions about the therapist's competence are explored rather than deplored. When the involuntary patient before us begins to see that we feel we are an imperfect and vulnerable human being and therefore more similar to him or her than different, treatment has a chance of working.

In the treatment of sexually exploitative clinicians who are not self-referred, it is well to keep in mind, particularly at the beginning of their therapeutic contact with us, that they will often deny they have been sexually involved with a patient or patients. Experienced practitioners have long recognized when a child has been referred for therapy by a parent, or a spouse has been pressured to seek counseling by a mate, these prospective patients frequently deny that they have inter-personal problems. Often they project their difficulties onto those who have referred them for treatment and say, "They are the sick ones!"

The difficulties that are involved for children or spouses who are pressured to go into psychotherapy are intensified for sexually exploitative therapists when they become patients. Not

only do they feel the same sense of embarrassment, vulnerability, defeat, and resentment that other involuntary patients
tend to experience, but also they have to appear before another
professional while their own professional license and other
symbols of professional expertise may soon be forfeited or have
been forfeited already. In many ways they feel themselves to be
third-class citizens!

When treating involuntary patients who have been accused
of acting unethically or illegally, we have to regard all of their
denials as resistances to therapy and not attempt to refute their
protestations. Once we imply that we are experiencing our
prospective patient as a distorter of the truth, we have alienated
the patient, have become his or her enemy, and can no longer
administer effective therapy. We have to remind ourselves
continually that when patients resist treatment, they are
protecting themselves against real or imagined dangers.

Patients who deny the truth often stir up strong and usually
negative countertransference reactions in us. They have a
tendency to puncture our omnipotent fantasies as they try to
manipulate us. To bolster our weakened self-esteem we are
often tempted to attack these patients by confronting them with
the real truth. When we do this, these patients only strengthen
their resolve to deny the facts, and the possibility of further
treatment is seriously jeopardized.

OTHER COUNTERTRANSFERENCE PROBLEMS

The patients we are discussing are therapists, which makes us
therapists inclined to identify rather strongly with them and to
see ourselves in them. What happens to us when we see
ourselves in someone like a Ron, a Roslyn, a Bob, or an Al?

One way of coping with our identification with colleagues
who have sexually exploited their patients is by repressing,
denying, and suppressing our fantasies to sexually exploit our
own patients. Instead of addressing the conflicts that have gotten them into trouble and helping them resolve their difficulties,

we try to prove to ourselves and to them that we are much different from them. Covertly or overtly, we become superego figures to them and instead of treating them, we try to convince them of their improprieties—as if they did not know about their unethical and unprofessional behavior. However, this form of countertransference probably exists in all of us. It is not easy to acknowledge that in all of us is a hungry, angry child that would like to defy parental figures, supervisors, and mentors, and have sex with our patients. All of us feel some of the vulnerability, self-doubt, injured narcissism, and emotional pain that exists in the therapist who acts out some of the primitive fantasies we try to monitor.

Rather than face fantasies that are untherapeutic if carried out into action, many of us defend against consciously experiencing the affects, thoughts, and wishes that activate erotic fantasies toward our patients. When we employ this type of "counter-transference defense" (Strean, 1993), we do not want to empathize with our patients. Instead, we seek distance from them, either through our subtle criticism or disinterest.

When we seek distance from patients in any form, our patients usually become quite sensitive to our behavior and do feel rejected. They can handle their feelings of rejection by rejecting us and quitting treatment or they can become repeatedly involved in negative therapeutic reactions and never resolve their conflicts.

In contrast to the countertransference reaction just addressed, there is another one in which we become overidentified with our sexually abusing patients and vicariously participate in their acting-out behavior. Under the guise of becoming a benign superego figure who is offering a corrective emotional experience to them, we encourage our patients to tell us all of the details of their sexual exploits, rationalize their behavior for them, and do not examine the feelings and fantasies that propelled their behavior and which, in most cases, activated their guilt about it.

When we do not explore fantasies or memories but subtly condone behavior, when we forgive without analyzing transference reactions or exposing resistances and conflicts, we are probably deriving some form of vicarious pleasure from our patients' provocative behavior. We are failing to note the pain they are causing themselves and their patients. In effect, we are colluding with the therapist-patient to continue the sexual exploitation of patients.

MAJOR TREATMENT PRINCIPLES

If we are able to monitor our countertransference problems and not feel or be too indulgent or critical with the patient under consideration, treatment can be effective in many cases and is not uniquely different from the therapy we offer most patients. But there are a few qualifications that should be addressed.

As the reader is now well aware, the theoretical approach utilized with the therapist-patients described in this book is classically Freudian. This implies that the patient's transference reactions and resistances are the focus of much of the work, and the practitioner's countertransference reactions and counter-resistances receive considerable analysis, either alone or in supervision. Attempts are made to make the unconscious conscious through the analysis of the patient's dreams, fantasies, and revived memories. The treatment described in this book adheres to the notion that the patient's history is constantly being revived in his or her current life and in the transference to the therapist. One of the objectives of the treatment is to help the patient see how and why his or her history is constantly being recapitulated everywhere (Fine, 1982; Freud, 1914; Strean, 1979, 1990).

Another principle of the psychotherapy that has been reiterated in this book is that the therapist should attempt to be neutral about the patient's behavior and associations as much as possible (A. Freud, 1946; Schafer, 1983). He or she should remain equidistant between id, ego, and superego. By this we mean that the therapist does not champion the gratification of id wishes, repudiate certain behavior of the patient, or rationalize and reinforce certain of the patient's defenses. Rather, the therapist attempts to show patients how and why they behave and feel the way they do. In so doing, the therapist hopes to help patients come as close as they can to the "analytic ideal" as proposed by Reuben Fine (1982). This means the "therapist-patient" will become more loving and less hateful, have a mature sex life, have realistic pleasure, experience a wide range of emotions, communicate well, and have a role in the family and community.

Cautionary Notes About Treating the Sexually Exploitative Clinician

Utilizing the above framework of psychotherapy, what are some of the cautionary notes that can be provided to the practitioner who works with the sexually exploitative clinician?

1. It has already been pointed out that many of the therapists who sexually abuse their patients come to us involuntarily. Consequently, they need a great deal of our time and patience when they deride psychotherapy, question our qualifications, and deny their sexual involvement with patients.

The resistances that we ascribed to the involuntary patient can also be applied to the voluntary patients such as the ones discussed in the previous chapters. As you will recall, many times Ron, Roslyn, Bob, and Al had a great deal of difficulty acknowledging their sexual acting out with patients; they needed considerable help before they could feel safe enough to discuss their sexual escapades with patients and the motives, fantasies, history, and other variables that gave rise to them.

2. As most clinicians realize, when patients are greeted by an empathetic and nonjudgmental listener, their tensions are released, their self-esteem rises, and they feel loved by what appears to be a benign parental figure. When this "honeymoon phase" of treatment (Fine, 1982) takes place, it usually occurs somewhere between the third month and first year of therapy. Because of their strong hunger for love, sexually exploitative practitioners often improve very dramatically during this period

because they feel more attended to than ever before and believe that no person has ever been quite so wonderful to them as the therapist appears to be.

It is important for the practitioner working with these therapist-patients to keep in mind that no honeymoon lasts forever. Consequently, despite the fact that the therapist-patients have seen the error of their ways, have stopped acting out sexually, have resolved many conflicts and given up many symptoms, the honeymoon phase should be seen as a temporary state with a cessation of symptoms and not as a permanent state of being—they are not "cured."

Many practitioners of different theoretical persuasions assume that if a patient gets better within a short period of time, this improvement is an enduring one. It rarely is! The bliss that is felt on any honeymoon in marriage or in therapy is a momentary event and should not be interpreted otherwise. This is particularly important for the treatment of the sexually acting-out therapist, who has a strong tendency to distort the meaning of bliss thinking it can be ever-present, only to be very disappointed later. Although we should not try to stop our therapist-patients from feeling pleased with themselves, their treatment, or with us during the honeymoon phase, we should not assume that treatment is over after a short period of time. When our attitude is one that implies "the honeymoon" is only a phase of treatment, this perspective is usually communicated to the patient and he or she continues the therapeutic trek with us, a little let down, but still hopeful.

3. Every treatment process contains one or more crises and the first one usually occurs "after the honeymoon is over." Sooner or later, every patient, like every honeymooner, recognizes that the partner cannot provide all that one fantasizes. Patients eventually recognize that the therapist cannot bestow permanent bliss, enduring love, and forever be a need-gratifying parent. This recognition by the patient then induces keen disappointment. He or she feels intense rage and often wishes to flee the treatment.

The first treatment crisis is particularly painful for the

therapist-patients under examination. Starved for love all of their lives, constantly trying to possess an omnipotent, all loving and giving partner, their feelings of letdown are extremely strong. Often they become very depressed and their wish to quit treatment can become a prolonged issue in therapy.

When the practitioner is aware of what the therapist-patient is experiencing during the first treatment crisis as well as during subsequent ones, it is helpful for the therapist-patient to hear from the practitioner. The practitioner should show the troubled patient that he or she knows how very disappointed the patient is. The therapist-patients that we are trying to help psycho-therapeutically feel comforted and better understood when they are told that all of their lives they had hoped to find a loving person who would always be there for them, thought the current therapist was that person, and now are seeing and feeling otherwise!

Crises occur quite frequently with these therapist-patients. So often their hopes are dashed, their wishes frustrated, and their narcissism punctured. When we work with them, as was noted in the treatment of Ron, Roslyn, Bob, and Al, we have to permit them to hate us for long periods of time and not retaliate.

Although the practitioner working with sexually abusing therapists in treatment does try to be a benign superego, as we saw with the subjects of our research, the practitioner's sincerity is frequently questioned. The patient often finds it difficult to believe that the practitioner does not want to heap scorn or deride the patient, but merely wants to understand him or her as well as possible. The patient's superego is usually much more punitive than the therapist's; but the patient usually needs a long time before he or she can grasp this difference. That is why many crises evolve throughout the treatment of the therapist-patients under study. His or her punitive superego is frequently asserting itself and is constantly being projected onto the therapist who, in the patient's mind, is almost always ready to "let the axe fall."

4. Although almost all patients in therapy progress and regress at various times, the patients with whom we are concerned

are much more dramatic and intense about it. As we have already observed, the ecstacy and bliss they feel during the honeymoon phase of therapy are stronger than in other patients and the depressed, angry aftermath is also more powerful.

These patients have a strong tendency to regress. In many ways they are fixated babies, preoccupied with preoedipal and pregenital concerns. Consequently, when they are or feel frustrated in the treatment and/or elsewhere, they long to be taken care of and yearn for the perfect breast. As we saw in the treatment of the subjects of this study, they appeared like hungry, helpless, demanding babies in many therapeutic sessions and it was crucial to their treatment to respect their frequent regressive displays without appearing to censure them.

Just as practitioners have to be patient and not pressuring when these patients regress deeply and frequently, they also have to recognize that the therapist-patients can exaggerate their progress, appear extremely expansive at times, and believe they are swiftly marching forward toward the Garden of Eden. At these times, the best way to help them is to be quiet but interested. When patients are overstimulated and excited, they need nonstimulating therapists who are relatively calm. The calm attitude often helps the patients who appear manic to "calm down" and start to explore the meaning of their feelings, thoughts and memories.

5. Although extratherapeutic contacts are sometimes inevitable (Strean, 1982), sexually acting-out therapists not only want them with their patients, but with their own therapists as well. As we have observed throughout this study, one of the major factors moving the therapist to have sex with the patient is a strong wish for a symbiotic attachment. This wish re-emerges when the sexually acting-out therapist becomes the recipient of treatment.

One way that the therapist-patient tries to gratify the wish for symbiotic merger is by arranging for extratherapeutic contacts with the therapist. This can take the form of making phone calls in between sessions, prolonging the therapeutic hours with chit-chat, and trying to be present in situations where the therapist is, such as at seminars, meetings, or conferences. Because therapists often share the same friends and colleagues, it is not an infrequent happenstance for a therapist-patient to arrange to meet his or her therapist socially.

It is imperative that every time the sexually exploitative therapist wants to or tries to arrange an extratherapeutic contact with us, the wishes, fantasies, anxieties, defenses, and conflicts that propel the desire in the patient should be thoroughly analyzed. The patient's wish for extratherapeutic contact should rarely be gratified. One of the best gifts an acting-out patient can receive from the therapist is a therapeutic attitude that consists of timely and tactful explorations, confrontations, clarifications, and interpretations. One of the worst things that an acting-out patient can receive from the therapist is the latter's collusion in an extratherapeutic contact.

Because the patient before us is so hungry for contact, conscious and unconscious attempts to see us outside the office are many. When we try to analyze with the patient his or her wish to relate to us other than as patient to therapist, we are not going to be loved. On the contrary! The patient will feel very frustrated, rageful, and revengeful. However, if we are clear about the therapeutic boundaries and nondefensive and nonretaliatory when we are the recipient of his or her rages, the patient slowly but surely will welcome our appropriate therapeutic attitude and move on in the therapy.

In many ways, exploring our patient's wishes to see us extratherapeutically, rather than colluding and having outside contacts, is providing the weaning that this infantile individual strongly needs. Like the mature parent who empathizes with the infant's anger at being weaned but does not submit to the baby's manipulations and demands, our approach to our patient should contain a similar attitude.

6. Just as the therapist-patient frequently progresses and regresses more than most patients do, he or she threatens to leave treatment more often. When we recognize that the individual we are treating has a fragmented ego with much weakness in several ego functions—object relations, frustration

tolerance, impulse control, and reality testing—it should not surprise us that this patient would want to get rid of us as soon as we do not gratify him or her. Very often this type of patient tries to provoke us to get rid of him or her, rather than dismissing us, as was shown by at least two of the subjects in this study.

In addition to helping the man or woman before us get in touch with the disappointments, frustrations, and revenge that are almost always part of his or her wish to end treatment, it is helpful to this patient to see that we are not going to stop the treatment, no matter how much we are provoked. This attitude can be very reassuring to the therapist-patient who feels unwanted and believes that being dismissed by us can occur almost at any time.

PREVENTIVE MEASURES

The major focus of the book concerns the psychodynamics and treatment of the therapist who has sexual contacts with patients. However, a few thoughts may be in order on what mental health professionals and organizations can do to lessen the frequency of sexual acting out between therapists and patients and to diminish the enormous damage inflicted on the parties involved.

Although the sexual dimension of the human being is much more appreciated by mental health professionals today than heretofore, the mental health professional's own sexuality as it is experienced in the therapeutic situation still receives insufficient attention.

One of the main ways that sexual exploitation of patients in psychotherapy can be reduced immeasurably is by recognizing that the therapist's wish to have sex with patients, particularly with those of the opposite sex, is an acceptable, natural, and probably universal desire that emerges in all of us who do psychotherapy. When prospective therapists in schools of social work, psychology departments, or residency programs in psychiatry are helped to acknowledge their essential human-ness, they will be less likely to want to rebel against their mentors and act out something that seems mysterious and is rarely discussed—sexual feelings toward patients.

It would also be extremely helpful to candidates in psycho-therapy and psychoanalytic training programs to have more courses and seminars on countertransference issues in general (Strean, 1993) and with a specific focus on sexualized trans-ference-countertransference reactions. When candidates are trained to look for their own erotic feelings and fantasies as they emerge in the clinical situation, and to talk about them with peers and mentors, acting out will be less likely to occur. As we have seen in child rearing and in living and working with teenagers, when sex is a more discussed and less tabooed issue, sexual acting out recedes.

Another way that we can reduce sexual exploitation of patients is by structuring our training programs in a way so that those being trained to be mental health professionals do not constantly witness their mentors breaking barriers (Greenacre, 1966). There is much socializing between mental health educators and their students. Four national studies have yielded data about sexual intimacies between educators and students and in all four, 10% to 15% of the students reported having sexual contacts with faculty members (Pope, 1989b).

It would appear that faculty members in psychotherapy training programs should be helped more extensively and intensively to view themselves as role models. Consequently, what they say and do with students in the classroom and outside of it, in supervision and outside of it, should be considered by them to be something planned and monitored, similar to what a clinician does in a disciplined therapeutic situation. When psychotherapy and psychoanalytic candidates in training consistently observe that their mentors are benign but not seductive, knowledgable but not imposing, supportive but not indulgent, they begin to experience them as ego ideals who are to be emulated in a positive manner, a manner that will enhance their patients' maturational processes. This will help to reverse a trend that began with Freud, whereby analyst and analysand, therapist and patient, work side by side (for example, Ferenczi and Jones, Freud and his inner circle, including his daughter Anna, who was also his analysand) and manipulate and frequently exploit one another (Grosskurth, 1991).

In many ways psychoanalytic and psychotherapeutic training institutes have emerged into political establishments with party lines, in-groups and out-groups, gurus and the like. This has led the eminent psychoanalyst and writer Roy Schafer (1992) to suggest that in certain respects theory is a political matter as is the selection of some training analysts and the selection and progression of candidates. He implies that "analytic power politics" play an important role in analytic education.

Because training institutes do become frequently like political parties and/or extended neurotic families, they provoke situations that involve a candidate's becoming a favored or disfavored son or daughter by someone high in the political or familial hierarchy. Being an extremely loved or hated son or daughter in a training institute does not promote maturity in the candidate. Rather, it tends to promote the possibility of the candidate acting out with his or her patients. Since they have been indulged, these candidates want to indulge. As they have not been adequately helped to control and monitor their own sexual impulses, they cannot help their patients control and monitor sexual impulses.

Schafer (1992) contends that the atmosphere in training institutes and the difficulties they engender too often makes a successful therapeutic experience a virtual impossibility for a candidate. States Schafer:

> I believe...that difficulties in analysis may become insurmountable when the stimulus of circumstance is unusually strong or prolonged, for then there is, in the analysand's psychic reality, so much seduction, hostility, and deprivation in the analytic relationship and, as a consequence, so much reason to cling to primitive defensive strategies, that even the most patient and clever

interpretive work makes no evident headway against a candidate's transference and defensive moves. (p. 255)

At a time when sexual exploitation is the leading cause of all professional practice litigation—an era when 87% of surveyed psychotherapists acknowledge feeling sexually attracted to their patients (Gabbard, 1989)—it would appear that part of the solution to this serious problem would be better training programs and better treatment for all of those who wish to be responsible and caring mental health professionals.

References

Abend, S. (1982). Serious illness in the analyst: Countertransference considerations. *Journal of the American Psychoanalytic Association, 30,* 365–379.

Abend, S. (1989). Countertransference and psychoanalytic technique. *The Psychoanalytic Quarterly, 58,* 374–396.

Adler, J. & Rosenberg, D. (1992). Dr. Bean and her little boy. *Newsweek Magazine,* April 13, 1992, pp. 56–57.

Akamatsa, T. (1988). Intimate relationships with former clients: National survey of attitudes and behavior among practitioners. *Professional Psychology: Research and Practice, 19,* 454–458.

Alexander, F. (1961). *The scope of psychoanalysis.* New York: Basic Books.

American Association for Marriage and Family Therapy (1988). AAMFT code of ethical principles for marriage and family therapists. Washington, DC.

Anzieu, D. (1986). *Freud's self analysis.* New York: International Universities Press.

Apfel, R. & Simon, B. (1986). Sexualized therapy: Causes and consequences. In A. Burgess & C. Hartman (Eds.), *Sexual exploitation of patients by health professionals* (pp. 143–151). New York: Praeger.

Appelbaum, P. & Jorgenson, L. (1991). Psychotherapist-patient sexual contact after termination of treatment: An analysis and a proposal. *American Journal of Psychiatry, 148,* 1466–1473.

Arlow, J. (1972). Some dilemmas in psychoanalytic education. *Journal of the American Psychoanalytic Association, 20,* 556–566.

Baranger, M. (1983). Process and non-process in analytic work. *International Journal of Psychoanalysis, 64,* 1–15.

Barnhouse, R. (1978). Sex between patient and therapist. *Journal of the American Academy of Psychoanalysis, 6,* 533–546.

Bates, C. & Brodsky, A. (1989). *Sex in the therapy hour: A case of professional incest.* New York: Guilford Press.

Baudry, F. (1991). The relevance of the analyst's character and attitudes to his work. *Journal of the American Psychoanalytic Association, 39,* 917–938.

Beck, M. (1992). Sex and psychotherapy. *Newsweek Magazine,* April 13, 1992, pp. 53–57.

Bergler, E. (1960). *Divorce won't help.* New York: Liveright Publishing Corporation.

Bergler, E. (1963). Marriage and divorce. In H. Herma & G. Kurth (Eds.), *A handbook of psychoanalysis*. Cleveland: World Publishing Company.

Bermak, G. (1977). Do psychiatrists have special emotional problems? *American Journal of Psychoanalysis, 37P,* 141–146.

Bion, W. (1962). Learning from experience. London: Heinemann.

Blum, H. (1973). The concept of the eroticized transference. *Journal of the American Psychoanalytic Association, 21,* 61–76.

Blum, H. (1986). Countertransference: Concepts and controversies. In A.D. Richards & M.S. Willick (Eds.), *Psychoanalysis: The science of mental conflict. Essays in honor of Charles Brenner* (pp. 229–243). Hillsdale, NJ: The Analytic Press.

Boesky, D. (1990). The psychoanalytic process and its components. *The Psychoanalytic Quarterly, 59,* 550–584.

Bouhoutsos, J. (1983). Sexual intimacy between psychotherapists and patients. *Professional Psychology Research and Practice, 14,* 185–196.

Bowlby, J. (1951). *Maternal care and mental health.* Geneva: World Health Organization.

Breedlove, W. & Breedlove, J. (1964). *Swap clubs: A study in contemporary sexual mores.* Los Angeles: Sherbourne Press.

Brenner, C. (1985). Countertransference as compromise formation. *The Psychoanalytic Quarterly, 54,* 155–163.

Brill, H. (1965). Psychiatric diagnosis, nomenclature, and classification. In B. Wolman (Ed.), *Handbook of Clinical Psychology.* New York: McGraw-Hill.

Brodsky, A. (1989). Sex between patient and therapist: Psychology's data and response. In G. Gabbard (Ed.), *Sexual exploitation in professional relationships* (pp. 15–26). Washington, DC: American Psychiatric Press.

Burton, A. (1972). *Twelve therapists.* San Francisco: Jossey-Bass.

Butler, S. & Zelen, S. (1977). Sexual intimacies between therapists and patients. *Psychotherapy: Theory, Research, and Practice, 14,* 139–145.

Buunk, B. & Driel, B. (1989). *Variant lifestyles and relationships.* Newbury Park, CA: Sage.

Celenza, A. (1991). The misuse of countertransference love in sexual intimacies between therapists and patients. *Psychoanalytic Psychology, 8,* 501–510.

Chesler, P. (1972). *Women and madness.* New York: Avon Books.

Chused, J. & Raphling, D. (1991). The analyst's mistakes. *Journal of the American Psychoanalytic Association, 40,* 89–116.

Chused, J. (1992). The patient's perception of the analyst: The hidden transference. *The Psychoanalytic Quarterly, 61,* 161–184.

Claman, J. (1987). Mirror hunger in the psychodynamics of sexually abusing therapists. *American Journal of Psychoanalysis, 47,* 35–40.

Clark, R. (1980). *Freud: The man and the cause.* New York: Random House.

Coen, S. (1981). Sexualization as a predominant mode of defense. *Journal of the American Psychoanalytic Association, 29,* 893–920.

Conte, H., Plutchik, R., Picard, S. & Karasu, T. (1989). Ethics in the practice of psychotherapy: A survey. *American Journal of Psychotherapy, 43,* 32–42.

Dahlberg, C. (1970). Sexual contact between patient and therapist. *Contemporary Psychoanalysis, 6,* 107–124.

DeMause, L. (1981). *Foundations of psychohistory.* New York: Creative Roots Press.

Deutsch, C. (1984). Self-reported sources of stress among psychotherapists. *Professional Psychology, 15,* 833–845.

Dohrenwend, B. & Dohrenwend, P. (1969). *Social stress and psychological disorder.* New York: Wiley.

Durbin, K. (1977). On sexual jealousy. In G. Clanton & L. Smith (Eds.), *Jealousy.* Englewood Cliffs, NJ: Prentice-Hall.

Eckhardt, M. (1978). Organizational schisms in American psychoanalysis. In J. Ivan & E. Carlson (Eds.), *American psychoanalysis: Origins and development* (pp. 141–161). New York: Brunner/Mazel.

Edelwich, J. & Brodsky, A. (1991). *Sexual dilemmas for the helping professional* (revised and expanded edition). New York: Brunner/Mazel.

Erikson, E. (1950). *Childhood and society.* New York: W.W. Norton.

Erikson, E. (1964). *Insight and responsibility: Lectures on the ethical implications of psychoanalytic insight.* New York: W.W. Norton.

Faludi, S. (1992). *Backlash.* New York: Crown.

Feldman, Y. (1958). A casework approach toward understanding parents of emotionally disturbed children. *Social Work, 3,* 23–29.

Felton, J. (1984). A psychoanalytic perspective on sexually open relations. *The Psychoanalytic Review, 71,* 279–295.

Fenichel, O. (1945). *The psychoanalytic theory of neurosis.* New York: W.W. Norton.

Fincham, F. & Bradbury, T. (1990). *The psychology of marriage: Basic issues and applications.* New York: Guilford.

Fine, R. (1975). *Psychoanalytic psychology.* New York: Jason Aronson.

Fine, R. (1981). *The psychoanalytic vision.* New York: The Free Press.

Fine, R. (1982). *The healing of the mind* (second edition). New York: The Free Press.

Fine, R. (1984). Countertransference reactions to the difficult patient. *Current Issues in Psychoanalytic Practice, 1,* 7–22.

Fine, R. (1990). *The history of psychoanalysis* (second edition). New York: Continuum.

Finell, J. (1985). Narcissistic problems in analysts. *International Journal of Psychoanalysis, 66,* 433–445.

Firestein, S. (1978). *Termination in psychoanalysis.* New York: International

Universities Press.

Frayn, D. & Silberfeld, M. (1986). Erotic transferences. *Canadian Journal of Psychiatry, 31,* 323–327.

Freeman, L. & Roy, J. (1976). *Betrayal.* New York: Stein and Day.

Freud, A. (1946). *The ego and the mechanisms of defense.* New York: International Universities Press.

Freud, A. (1965). *Normality and pathology in childhood: Assessment of development.* New York: International Universities Press.

Freud, S. (1896). Further remarks on the neuro-psychoses of defense. *Standard Edition of the Complete Psychological Works (Vol. 3).* London: Hogarth Press.

Freud, S. (1905). Three essays on the theory of sexuality. *Standard Edition of the Complete Psychological Works (Vol. 7).* London: Hogarth Press.

Freud, S. (1910). The future prospects of psycho-analytic therapy. *Standard Edition of the Complete Psychological Works (Vol. 11).* London: Hogarth Press.

Freud, S. (1914). Remembering, repeating, and working through. *Standard Edition of the Complete Psychological Works (Vol. 12).* London: Hogarth Press.

Freud, S. (1915). Observations on transference love. *Standard Edition of the Complete Psychological Works (Vol. 12).* London: Hogarth Press.

Freud, S. (1916). Some character types met with in psychoanalytic work. *Standard Edition of the Complete Psychological Works (Vol. 16).* London: Hogarth Press.

Freud, S. (1923). The ego and the id. *Standard Edition of the Complete Psychological Works (Vol. 19).* London: Hogarth Press.

Freudenberger, H. & Robbins, A. (1979). The hazards of being a psychoanalyst. *The Psychoanalytic Review, 66,* 275–296.

Frosch, J. (1991). The New York psychoanalytic civil war. *Journal of the American Psychoanalytic Association, 39,* 1037–1064.

Gabbard, K. & Gabbard, G. (1987). *Psychiatry and the cinema.* Chicago: University of Chicago Press.

Gabbard, G. (1989). *Sexual exploitation in professional relationships.* Washington, DC: American Psychiatric Press.

Gabbard, G. (1991). Sexual misconduct by female therapists: The love cure fantasy. *The Psychodynamic Letter, 1* (6), 1–3.

Gay, P. (1988). *Freud: A life for our time.* New York: W.W. Norton.

Gaylin, W. (1976). *Caring.* New York: Alfred A. Knopf.

Gediman, H. (1991). Seduction trauma: Complemental intrapsychic and interpersonal perspectives on fantasy and reality. *Psychoanalytic Psychology, 8* (4), 381–402.

Gelinas, D. (1983). The persisting negative effects of incest. *Psychiatry, 46,* 312–332.

Glover, E. (1960). *The roots of crime*. New York: International Universities Press.

Goldberg, C. (1986). *On being a psychotherapist: The journey of the healer*. New York: Gardner Press.

Greenacre, P. (1966). Problems of training analysis. *Psychoanalytic Quarterly, 35*, 540–567.

Greenbaum, H. (1975). The psychological impact of the sexual revolution. In E. Edelson (Ed.), *Sexuality and psychoanalysis* (pp. 291–305). New York: Brunner/Mazel.

Greenson, R. (1967). *The technique and practice of psychoanalysis*. New York: International Universities Press.

Griffin, N. (1992). *The selected letters of Bertrand Russell, Vol. 1: The private years, 1884–1914*. Boston: Houghton Mifflin.

Grinberg, L. (1968). On acting out and its role in the psychoanalytic process. *International Journal of Psychoanalysis, 49*, 171–178.

Grinstein, A. (1980). *Sigmund Freud's dreams*. New York: International Universities Press.

Grosskurth, P. (1991). *The secret ring*. New York: Addison-Wesley.

Guy, J. & Liaboe, G. (1985). Suicide among psychotherapists: Review and discussion. *Professional Psychology: Research and Practice, 16*, 470–472.

Harlow, H. (1974). *Learning to love*. New York: Jason Aronson.

Hartmann, H. (1964). Essays on ego psychology. New York: International Universities Press.

Hendin, H. (1975). *The age of sensation*. New York: W.W. Norton.

Henry, W. (1971). *The fifth profession*. San Francisco: Jossey-Bass.

Henry, W. (1973). *The public and private lives of psychotherapists*. San Francisco: Jossey-Bass.

Herman, J., Gartrell, N., Olarte, S., Feldstein, M., & Localio, R. (1987). Psychiatrist-patient sexual contact: Results of a national survey of psychiatrists' attitudes. *American Journal of Psychiatry, 144*, 164–169.

Honigmann, J. (1944). A cultural theory of obscenity. *Journal of Criminal Psychopathology, 5*, 715–733.

Howard, J. (1978). *Families*. New York: Simon and Schuster.

Hull, J., Lane, R., & Okie, J. (1989). Sexual acting out and the desire for revenge. *The Psychoanalytic Review, 76*, 3: 313–328.

Hunt, M. (1974). *Sexual behavior in the 1970's*. New York: Dell.

Jacobs, T. (1986). On countertransference enactments. *Journal of the American Psychoanalytic Association, 34*, 289–307.

Jacobson, E. (1964). *The self and the object world*. New York: International Universities Press.

Jaques, E. (1976). *A general theory of bureaucracy*. New York: Halsted.

Jones, E. (1957). *The life and work of Sigmund Freud: The last phase (Vol. 3)*. New York: Basic Books.

Kadushin, C. (1969). *Why people go to psychiatrists.* New York: Atherton Press.

Kaplan, H. (1974). *The new sex therapy.* New York: Brunner/Mazel.

Kaplan, H. (1991). Greed: A psychoanalytic perspective. *The Psychoanalytic Review, 78* (4), 505–523.

Karasu, T. & Socarides, C. (1979). *On sexuality.* New York: International Universities Press.

Karasu, T., Rosenbaum, M., & Jerrett, I. (1979). Overview of new sex therapies. In T. Karasu & C. Socarides (Eds.), *On sexuality.* New York: International Universities Press.

Karasu, T. (1980). The ethics of psychotherapy. *American Journal of Psychiatry, 137,* 1502–1512.

Kardener, S. (1974). Sex and the physician-patient relationship. *American Journal of Psychiatry, 131,* 1134–1136.

Kernberg, O. (1986). Institutional problems of psychoanalytic education. *Journal of the American Psychoanalytic Association, 34,* 799–834.

Klein, M. (1957). *Envy and gratitude.* New York: Basic Books.

Kohut, H. (1977). *The restoration of the self.* New York: International Universities Press.

Kottler, J. (1986). *On being a therapist.* San Francisco: Jossey-Bass.

Kovel, J. (1976). *A complete guide to therapy.* New York: Pantheon Books.

Lane, R. (1990). *Psychoanalytic approaches to supervision.* New York: Brunner/Mazel.

Leighton, A. (1963). *The character of danger.* New York: Basic Books.

Leonard, L. (1983). *The wounded woman: Healing the father-daughter relationship.* Boston: Shambhala.

Love, S. & Mayer, H. (1970). Going along with defenses in resistive families. In H. Strean (Ed.), *New Approaches in Child Guidance.* Metuchen, NJ: Scarecrow Press.

Maeder, T. (1989). *Children of psychiatrists.* New York: Harper & Row.

Mahler, M. (1968). *On human symbiosis and the vicissitudes of individuation.* New York: International Universities Press.

Mahler, M., Pine, F., & Bergman, A. (1975). *The psychological birth of the infant.* New York: Basic Books.

Marmor, J. (1953). The feeling of superiority: An occupational hazard in the practice of psychotherapy. *American Journal of Psychiatry, 110,* 370–376.

Marmor, J. (1972). Sexual acting-out in psychotherapy. *American Journal of Psychoanalysis, 32,* 3–8.

Marmor, J. (1976). Some psychodynamic aspects of the seduction of patients in psychotherapy. *American Journal of Psychoanalysis, 36,* 319–323.

Masson, J. (1984). *The assault on truth: Suppression of the seduction theory.*

New York: Straus and Giroux.

Masson, J. (1985). *The complete letters of Sigmund Freud to Wilhelm Fliess, 1887–1904.* Cambridge, MA: Harvard University Press.

Masson, J. (1990). *Final analysis: The making and unmaking of a psychoanalyst.* Reading, MA: Addison-Wesley.

Masters, W. & Johnson, V. (1966). *The human sexual response.* Boston: Little, Brown.

Masters, W. & Johnson, V. (1970). *Human sexual inadequacy.* Boston: Little, Brown.

McCartney, J. (1966). Overt transference. *Journal of Sex Research, 2,* 227–237.

Menninger, K. (1957). Psychological factors in the choice of medicine as a profession. *Bulletin of the Menninger Clinic, 21,* 99–106.

Menninger, K. (1959). *A psychiatrist's world.* New York: Viking.

Menninger, K. & Holzman, P. (1973). *Theory of psychoanalytic technique* (second edition). New York: Basic Books.

Miller, A. (1981). *Prisoners of childhood.* New York: Basic Books.

Mintz, E. (1969). Time-extended marathon groups. *Psychotherapy: Theory, Research, and Practice, 6,* 232–234.

Moore, A. (1982). Well-being and the woman psychiatrist. *Journal of Psychiatric Treatment and Evaluation, 4,* 437–439.

Murstein, B. (1978). *Exploring intimate life styles.* New York: Springer.

Packard, V. (1968). *The sexual wilderness.* New York: David McKay.

Payne, R. (1973). *The life and death of Adolph Hitler.* New York: Praeger.

Person, E. (1983). Women in therapy: Therapist gender as a variable. *International Review of Psychoanalysis, 10,* 193–204.

Person, E. (1985). The erotic transference in women and in men: Differences and consequences. *Journal of the American Academy of Psychoanalysis, 13,* 159–180.

Plasil, E. (1985). *Therapist: The shocking autobiography of a woman sexually exploited by her analyst.* New York: St. Martin's Press.

Pope, K. (1986). Research and laws regarding therapist-patient sexual involvement: Implications for therapists. *American Journal of Psychotherapy, 40,* 564–571.

Pope, K., Tabachnik, B., & Keith-Spiegel, P. (1987). Ethics of practice: The beliefs and behaviors of psychologists as therapists. *The American Psychologist, 42,* 993–1006.

Pope, K. (1989a). Rehabilitation of therapists who have been sexually intimate with a patient. In G. Gabbard (Ed.), *Sexual exploitation in professional relationships.* Washington, DC: American Psychiatric Press.

Pope, K. (1989b). Teacher-student sexual intimacy. In G. Gabbard (Ed.), *Sexual exploitation in professional relationships.* Washington, DC: American Psychiatric Press.

Pope, K. & Vetter V. (1991). Prior therapist-patient sexual involvement among patients seen by psychologists. *Psychotherapy, 28* (3), 429–438.

Reik, T. (1941). Masochism in modern man. New York: Grove Press.

Rennie, T. (1962). *Mental health in the metropolis.* New York: McGraw-Hill.

Richardson, L. (1985). *The new other woman: Contemporary single women in affairs with married men.* New York: The Free Press.

Rosenfeld, A. (1979). Incidence of a history of incest among 18 female psychiatric patients. *American Journal of Psychiatry, 136,* 791–795.

Rutter, P. (1989). *Sex in the forbidden zone.* New York: Fawcett Crest.

Sachs, H. (1947). Observations of a training analyst. *Psychoanalytic Quarterly, 16,* 157–169.

Sachs, H. (1991). On the genesis of perversions (translated by R.B. Goldberg). *American Imago, 48* (3), 283–293.

Sandler, J. (1976). Countertransference and role responsiveness. *International Review of Psychoanalysis, 3,* 43–48.

Saul, L. (1976). *Psychodynamics of hostility.* New York: Jason Aronson.

Schafer, R. (1960). The loving and beloved superego in Freud's structural theory. *Psychoanalytic Study of the Child, 15,* 163–188. New York: International Universities Press.

Schafer, R. (1983). *The analytic attitude.* New York: Basic Books.

Schafer, R. (1992). *Retelling a life.* New York: Basic Books.

Scheflen, A. (1965). Quasi-courtship behavior in psychotherapy. *Psychiatry 28,* 245–257.

Searles, H. (1975). The patient as therapist to his analyst. In P. Giovacchini (Ed.), *Factors and techniques in psychoanalytic therapy, Vol. 2,* (pp. 95–195). New York: Jason Aronson.

Searles, H. (1979). *Countertransference and related subjects.* New York: International Universities Press.

Serban, G. (1981). Sexual activity in therapy: Legal and ethical issues. *American Journal of Psychotherapy, 35,* 76–85.

Sexton, L., & Ames, L. (1991). *Anne Sexton: A self-portrait in letters.* New York: Houghton-Mifflin.

Shainess, N. (1979). Gender stereotypes, identity, sexual concepts, and behavior today. In M. Nelson & J. Ikenberry (Eds.), *Psychosexual Imperatives.* New York: Human Science Press.

Shapiro, D. (1976). The analyst's own analysis. *Journal of the American Psychoanalytic Association, 24,* 5–42.

Sheehy, G. (1992). *The silent passage.* New York: Random House.

Shepard, M. (1971). *The love treatment: Sexual intimacy between patients and psychotherapists.* New York: Peter Wyden.

Sigman, M. (1985). The parallel process phenomenon in the supervisory relationship—A therapist's view. *Current Issues in Psychoanalytic Practice, 2,* 21–31.

Sipe, A.W.R. (1990). *A secret world: Sexuality and the search for celibacy.* New York: Brunner/Mazel.

Slakter, E. (1987). *Countertransference.* Northvale, NJ: Jason Aronson.

Smith, J. & Smith, L. (1974). *Beyond monogamy.* Baltimore, MD: The Johns Hopkins University Press.

Smith, S. (1989). The seduction of the female patient. In G. Gabbard (Ed.), *Sexual exploitation in professional relationships* (pp. 57–59). Washington, DC: American Psychiatric Press.

Spencer, J. (1978). Father-daughter incest. *Child Welfare, 57,* 581–590.

Spotnitz, H. & Freeman, L. (1964). *The wandering husband.* Englewood Cliffs, NJ: Prentice-Hall.

Steinem, G. (1992). *Revolution from within.* Boston: Little, Brown.

Sternbach, O. (1947). Arrested ego development and its treatment in conduct disorders and neuroses of childhood. *The Nervous Child, 6,* 306–317.

Stolorow, R. & Atwood, G. (1979). *Faces in a cloud: Subjectivity in personality theory.* New York: Jason Aronson.

Strean, H. (1975). *Personality theory and social work practice.* Metuchen, NJ: The Scarecrow Press.

Strean, H. (1976). *Crucial issues in psychotherapy.* Metuchen, NJ: The Scarecrow Press.

Strean, H. (1978). *Clinical social work.* New York: The Free Press.

Strean, H. (1979). *Psychoanalytic theory and social work practice.* New York: The Free Press.

Strean, H. (1980). *The extramarital affair.* New York: The Free Press.

Strean, H. (1982). *Controversy in psychotherapy.* Metuchen, NJ: The Scarecrow Press.

Strean, H. (1983). *The sexual dimension: A guide for the helping professional.* New York: The Free Press.

Strean, H. (1988). Effects of childhood sexual abuse on the psychosocial functioning of adults. *Social Work, 33,* 465–467.

Strean, H. (1990). *Resolving resistances in psychotherapy.* New York: Brunner/Mazel.

Strean, H. (1991a). *Behind the Couch.* New York: Continuum.

Strean, H. (1991b). Colluding illusions among analytic candidates, their supervisors, and their patients: A major factor in some treatment impasses. *Psychoanalytic Psychology, 8,* 403–414.

Strean, H. (1993). *Resolving counterresistances in psychotherapy.* New York: Brunner/Mazel.

Streisand, B. (1992). Physicians, heal thyselves. *Newsweek.* June 29, 1992.

Strupp, H. (1977). *Psychotherapy for better or worse: The problem of negative effects.* New York: Jason Aronson.

Sullivan, H.S. (1953). *The interpersonal theory of psychiatry.* New York: W.W. Norton.

Sulloway, F. (1979). *Freud: Biologist of the mind.* New York: Basic Books.

Sussman, M. (1992). *A curious calling: Unconscious motivations for practicing psychotherapy.* New York: Jason Aronson.

Teitelbaum, S. (1990). Supertransference: The role of the supervisor's blind spots. *Psychoanalytic Psychology, 7,* 243–258.

Toffler, A. (1970). *Future shock.* New York: Random House.

Twemlow, S. & Gabbard, G. (1989). The lovesick therapist. In G. Gabbard (Ed.), *Sexual exploitation in professional relationships* (pp. 71–87). Washington, DC: American Psychiatric Press.

Walker, E. & Young, P. (1986). *A killing cure.* New York: Holt, Rinehart and Winston.

Weinshel, E. (1990). Further observations on the psychoanalytic process. *The Psychoanalytic Quarterly, 59,* 629–649.

Wheelis, A. (1958). *The quest for identity.* New York: W.W. Norton.

Williamson, D. (1977). Extramarital involvements in couple interaction. In R. Stahmann & W. Hiebert (Eds.), *Counseling in marital and sexual problems.* Baltimore, MD: Williams and Wilkins.

Zilbergeld, B. & Evans, M. (1980). The inadequacy of Masters and Johnson. *Psychology Today,* April, 1980, pp. 29–43.

Index